LIVING

IN

GRACE

Carolyn Ann Bardsley

LIVING IN GRACE

Copyright © 2016 by Carolyn Ann Bardsley

All Rights Reserved

ISBN-13: 978-1537681108

ISBN-10: 1537681109

Contents

Preface

This is my testimony of how I live in grace and how God has been faithful to fulfill His promises concerning His Spirit leading me from within my heart.

This book is a sequel to *GRACE: God's Divine Influence Upon Our Heart And His Expression In And Through Our Life*, which gives the Biblical foundations upon which my walk in grace is built.

I include what I have learned and experienced being led by God's Spirit. I hope this will encourage you to step out and live in grace.

I also include my hesitations and struggles to give up control and submit to God's Spirit within me.

I begin by explaining how I live in grace: God's divine influence upon my heart and His expression in and through me.

Chapter 1 is my testimony of how I let God have *His divine influence* in my life.

Chapter 2 shows how I permit God to *influence my heart* and how I maintain a heart relationship with God my Father.

Chapter 3 reveals the surprising results of God *expressing Himself in and through me* as I submit to Him.

Chapter 4 concludes with a warning about the opposition and persecution we can expect from law-based religious people. I discuss how they persecuted Jesus and His disciples and then give examples of opposition and persecution in my own life.

How God works with me may be different from how He works with you. We are all unique and God knows best what we need to draw closer to Him.

If you are already living in grace, I believe my testimony will encourage you to endure when you experience the unexpected losses associated with committing to the Lord. I believe if others had explained to me the losses I would encounter, I could have been better prepared to face the heart-wrenching times I suffered in regards to cherished relationships.

The stakes are high in this walk of faith, but the blessings are unimaginable and worth the losses of our worldly attachments.

This then is my witness of how I live grace: *God's divine influence upon my heart and His expression in and through my life.*

Carolyn Bardsley
June 2016

Chapter 1: Living Grace: God's Divine Influence On My Life

The first priority in walking in grace is to submit to God's Spirit in our heart and to believe that He is leading us from within our heart.

Giving Up Control to God's Spirit

To remind myself that I am no longer the independent self I used to be, I begin each day by asking God to be LORD of my life. I ask Him to fill me with His Spirit and to express Himself in and through me. I present my body a living sacrifice to Him so that He can be in charge of my life.

I believe that God is loving and faithful and that He comes when I submit to Him. He honors a humble heart.

I do this every day to assure myself, not to remind God. I am sure God remembers. I am the one who so easily forgets. Many days I repeat this prayer during the day because I inadvertently take back control of my life or allow others to control me.

I know I always retain the power to choose whom I will follow and obey, so I reaffirm my covenant with the Lord humbly recognizing my own sinful nature that desires independence and control. I realize I am weak and I must rely on God's Spirit in me to keep me from straying. All He needs is my permission, so I give it to Him each day. I do this at least once a day because He asks me to live one day at a time and not to presume on tomorrow.

1

I realize that God is not so much interested in my works as He is in accomplishing His works in and through me. He wants my availability, not my ability. God designed us to have His Spirit in charge. Works we do to impress Him are not what He desires. He desires oneness with us and asks us to work together with Him. When we make God our divine influence, our works become God's works because we give Him permission to reign in us and through us.

For much of my life I have tried to accomplish for God—so much of it was based on beliefs from Scripture about church attendance, tithing, helping others, reading the Bible, and bringing others to Christ. As I look back over my self-righteousness, I can see that these tasks are the same in all religions. These are the works the Pharisees were so proud of and gave them perceived elevated status. Jesus repeatedly rebuked them for their works and Paul wrote letters rebuking the early Christians who reverted to works and away from faith and grace. In my zealousness to please my LORD I can revert to BELIEFS and WORKS rather than BELIEVING in my LIVING LORD within and His divine influence upon my heart and HIS EXPRESSION in and through me.

Faith is required to do the works of God. We ask the Spirit of God to reign in our lives and then trust that God will in fact work in and through us. We listen and follow what He speaks and shows us from within. We follow the motivations of our heart because we know who the resident of our heart is.

This requires FAITH on a magnitude that many do not embark on. It is so much easier to believe words written in a book and try to live them. We are so prone to this with our self-help psychology that we use the same principles in our religion. This is self-righteousness and is not Christ our righteousness. Only His presence in us and through us is righteousness.

All attempts to be righteous by living verses from Scripture are but Phariseeism in modern times. Christ would say the same things to us that He said to the Pharisees.

You search the scriptures, because you think that in them you have eternal life; and it is they that bear witness to me; yet you refuse to come to me that you may have life.
John 5:39-40

Perhaps you think you are not like the Pharisees. This works issue is not a small one and I see how easily I fall back into works of the law.

If you are not hearing God and following Him, then you are most likely doing works of the law. If you do not trust God's Spirit in your heart to lead and guide you then you are probably still operating under the law. You have not entered into the freedom of God's kingdom within.

Take stock of the works you do and see if you do them to please God. Often this is a big clue that we have severed ourselves from Christ to do works of the law. Often we quote Scripture to justify our works such as tithing, church attendance, and ministering to others. I have found that my ministry desires are often just another way that I consider myself to be above others based on my "good works" and has little to do with my faith in Christ in me. This is a hard pill to swallow, but until we are willing to give up good works and rely on God from within, we are choosing to be under the law and separated from Christ. Often what we volunteer to do in the church is motivated by feeling good about ourselves, looking good to others, and seeing ourselves as better than others. Much of this work is wasted and does more harm than good. When God is in charge, His works are not in vain.

Two Scriptures are particularly meaningful to me in giving up control to the LORD:

> **Seek FIRST the kingdom of God, and his righteousness;** *and all these things shall be added unto you.*
> *Matthew 6:33*

> *I appeal to you therefore, brethren, by the mercies of God, to* **present your bodies as a living sacrifice, holy and acceptable to God, which is your spiritual worship.** *Do not be conformed to this world but be transformed by the renewal of your mind,* **that you may prove what is the will of God, what is good and acceptable and perfect.**
> *Romans 12:1-2*

I present my body to the Lord each day in order that He can reign in me and set up His kingdom within me. His divine influence saves me. He does His work in me and through me.

Giving Up Control Is Not Abdication

When I first realized that God wanted to be in charge of my life, I misinterpreted it to mean that I gave up control and God did everything. I literally abdicated my life to God, meaning I did nothing and accepted everything that came into my life. In corporations, we call this delegating responsibilities upward.

Eventually I recognized this was not what God intends. He isn't looking for a passive robot to operate. God does not want us abdicating our life to Him.

God wants a relationship of oneness with us where we are active participants. God gave us the power of choice and He never takes that away from us. Our choice is to cooperate with Him by allowing Him to be the initiator. I didn't realize what it meant to give up control to the LORD and what it looked like.

What helped me see my irresponsibility was observing another abdicate to God. I watched her and saw that she attributed everything to God's will for her life. I could see that she was taking no responsibility for her life. She was creating the disasters and attributing them to God. This was not bringing glory to God and, I thought, giving God a bad reputation. Not only was she abdicating to God, she was depending on other Christians to support her. This was a wake up call for me. This showed me that some Christians believe God is in control, but it's an excuse for irresponsible behavior.

God in charge is better than our responsible behavior. He does a better job through us than we would do on our own. God designed us to be one with Him and to function as a unit with His Spirit within. We work together when we are submitted to Him. We have an active role.

He speaks and it is up to us to heed His words and do what He desires to do in and through us. He motivates us and it is up to us to obey and live from the motivations He puts on our heart. To do this we must abandon our plans and goals. We trust the LIVING LORD and SAVIOR within and let Him direct our life. He designed us to be one with Him and this is the purpose of Christ's dying on the cross and defeating the enemy. He reconciled us to our Father. To live any other way is to nullify the work of Christ.

God knows what is best for us. If we listen and obey, we can live the abundant life He promised in relationship with Him. We cannot check out and expect Him to do it all for us like a doting father. He asks us to listen to His voice and to obey.

As Jesus did only what the Father did and said, so we are to obey God's words and promptings. This is why it is so important to be able to hear His voice and to have our heart tender and receptive to His promptings.

This has motivated me to learn to hear God's voice and promptings and to have faith to step out and do what I believe He is saying and motivating me to do. This was not easy. Who likes to risk failure or look like a fool?

This was a great struggle for me, especially because those around me didn't believe God talked with people today and they believed that the heart was deceitful above all else. I knew if I did something stupid in my childlike walk of faith I would be ridiculed. I had been teaching others how to plan their careers and life, now I was thinking about letting God direct my life.

It was very scary, but the Lord was gentle and nurturing. He spent time explaining Scriptures to me and how they all pointed to Him and His desire to be Lord in my life. Repeatedly He would remind me how Jesus lived in relationship with Him.

I was surprised that God seemed more interested in my relationship with Him than what it was that I was to be doing. He seemed pleased to just spend time with me and patiently answer the multitude of questions I had about my faith.

This is why I encourage others to learn to hear God's voice because if we cannot hear His words how can we obey? I obeyed Bible verses before I could hear God's words directly to me. I now realize that living Bible verses was living under the law and negated what Christ had won for me. *Obeying the LIVING WORDS of our LIVING LORD is LIFE and LIVING IN GRACE.*

My Continual Need for Repentance

Most Christians believe that they have little need for repentance once they become a Christian, but repentance is not a one-time event.

I see repentance as an act of putting God in charge of my life. Christ restored me to God the Father, but I need to maintain my oneness relationship with God my Father.

I find myself reverting back to my old independent self and separating from God. I do this with my plans and schedules. I get so focused on completing tasks that I ignore the Lord's promptings. Sometimes I literally wear myself out before I realize that I am not in submission to my loving Father but under the control of the slave driver of this world.

I do this when I give myself away to another person and lose myself. I listen and follow the other person more than I listen to God's Spirit within me.

Repentance is returning to God and humbly submitting to His will again. Repentance is recognizing that I have returned to laws and beliefs and wandered from grace and His divine influence. I repent and turn around.

Repentance keeps me focused on the kingdom of God within me and being the temple of the LIVING God.

I used to ask for forgiveness and then find myself repeating the same sins. I discovered that my greatest need is to have God in charge. That requires repentance. Repentance focuses me on my need for God to be in charge. Forgiveness, on the other hand, seems to focus me on myself and what I need to do to not stray again. Forgiveness seems to point me to my own willpower and my need to take control to avoid erring again.

Majoring on repentance lessens my need for forgiveness. God in charge of my life is a sinless life, because God does not sin. Repentance eliminates the big SIN of separation from God so that I don't sin.

Repentance points me to God and my need to give up control. Repentance is the path to living grace.

No More Laws and Authorities Between Me and God

One of the most difficult changes for me to make was to come out from under all the laws and authorities I had created for myself.

I read the Bible and taught Bible studies for many years. I believe in reading the Bible as a daily practice, but I didn't realize that there are two decidedly different ways to read it.

My first approach to reading the Bible was to read verses and pick up beliefs making them laws that I tried to obey. I read the Bible to remind myself of all the commands I found there for living what I thought was a godly life. My self-will was determined to be "good" by doing this will of God. I literally took control and tried to carry out what I read. In addition, I would listen to sermons and read Christian books, which gave me more suggestions for what I should be doing to live a godly life. I readily picked up what others thought I should be doing, especially those I believed to be in spiritual authority over me. I had no difficulty following authority.

My second approach to reading the Bible is to recognize that it points to my LIVING LORD and SAVIOR and understand the relationship He wants to have with me.

The first approach led me away from the LORD by adding more laws to obey, causing me to take more control over my life. The second approach caused me to seek my LIVING LORD and pursue relationship with Him. The first way of reading the Bible produces a faith based on *beliefs*; the second creates and nurtures a faith based on *believing* in my LIVING LORD and SAVIOR.

Two experiences had a great impact on how I read the Bible and listen to spiritual authorities.

The first came when I was pondering on Christ's rebuke of the Pharisees, the religious people of His day. Jesus rebukes the

Pharisees for thinking that eternal life is in studying and obeying Scripture rather than coming to Him to have life. I thought I had already come to Christ. I had made my declaration of faith and believed I was a Christian. The phrase that bothered me was the contrast between reading Scripture and coming to Him. What did it mean to "come to Him"?

My second experience was in my Master's program where I interacted with people many of whom called themselves spiritual yet didn't acknowledge Christ. They would be what Christians might refer to as New Age. I watched as they read books for inspiration and thoughts for the day. I saw that they too had spiritual authorities they looked to for guidance. These observations caused me to reconsider how I read the Bible and listened to spiritual authorities. How was my faith different?

The Lord showed me that many religions and philosophies have books and spiritual authorities, but none has a LIVING SAVIOR within. God's emphasis on a LIVING SAVIOR WITHIN caught my attention.

It was then I realized my faith was in a LIVING being. God was alive. Christ was alive. How then did I relate to them? What was the purpose of Scripture and spiritual authorities?

Christ clearly states that the purpose of Scripture is to bring us to Him, not replace Him. Spiritual authorities too are to bring us to our LIVING LORD.

From then on, I considered Scripture a pointer to my LIVING LORD and SAVIOR. This was a totally different way of reading Scripture. Now I see how all Scriptures do indeed point to Christ.

As for spiritual authorities, I found few point me to the LORD and His LIVING presence in me. Most point me to beliefs and living under the law. I find that having God's Spirit in me and heeding His promptings, makes me aware of law-based sermons and Christian books that promote 'good works' by self-effort.

Now I am aware that it can be dangerous to follow a spiritual leader or the Bible. God wants us to have no other gods before Him, including Scripture and human authorities. He wants us to follow Him and Him alone.

Living in grace is giving God the Father our life and then following His Spirit from within.

No Longer Giving My Life Away to Others

From my Christian upbringing, I had been taught to give my life away to others. I was taught that loving others was giving up my life for them.

When I got serious about my faith and began reading the Bible I found Scriptures that I thought supported this belief. So it became even more ingrained in me. I was available to help anyone. My life was defined as helping others. All those verses about loving my neighbor as myself rang in my mind as the way to live. I remembered the Scripture that said there was no greater love than to lay down my life for another. The Good Samaritan was my role model.

When God began to teach me what it means to give my life to Him and follow Him, I had a dilemma. What did it mean to follow Him? Was I to continue responding to everyone who came into my life with a need? Was this following Him or following man? I wanted to be a good Christian and do what was right.

The Lord showed me that I had given my life to Him and that I was dead and had no *life* to give anyone else. This came as a shock to me, but I understood at some level what He was saying to me. I had given the LORD my life and wanted to do His will. I cannot have two masters.

He went on to explain that I was to love Him with my ALL and that meant to give Him my ALL. I had told Him I wanted to live this way and He was simply reminding me of my commitment to Him.

He went on to say that I am to love others *as* myself, but that this was the second commandment and that it followed the first commandment of loving Him with my ALL.

He told me that He was now in charge and that I am to listen and follow His leading from within and to not give to be giving. He showed me that He is the LOVE that I pass on to others and that I can only do this as He directs. I am not to come up with my own good works or respond to every need I see. He prompts me to meet certain needs and not others. My work is to believe in Him by listening and obeying. God showed me the difference between sharing my life with others and giving up my life to others.

God loves everyone and He is trying to woo everyone back to Himself. He is the only one who knows what is good for me and others. My assuming that I had to give to everyone was a lie and a way the enemy got me to give away my life. I believe I interfered many times with what God was doing in another's life. I was trying to save them from difficult situations, while God was trying to SAVE them. I was trying to make their life better so they could resume the life they were living. God was interested in changing their life to be conformed to His.

"My son, do not regard lightly the discipline of the Lord, nor lose courage when you are punished by him. **For the Lord disciplines him whom he loves, and chastises every son whom he receives."** *Hebrews 12:5-6*

Once when I was praying for God to cure my illness, the Lord asked me why I wanted to be cured. My immediate response was so that I could get back to running my business. I was surprised to hear Him say that He didn't want me to continue working so hard and that He wanted me to let Him work through me. Many of you are like me, we want God to fix our difficulties so we can resume our life, when He is trying to change our life.

As God has worked in my life using hurts and pains to bring me to Himself, I have become more at peace with what God has shown me about not giving my life away to others. I see loving others in a whole new light. LOVE has a new meaning to me. God Himself is LOVE and this is the LOVE I am to give to others. I am more able now to give up responsibilities for others that I had no business assuming.

Now I wait until the Lord motivates me or tells me to help. It is His work in and through me that will do good in the life of another. My own contribution most likely will not affect the other person in any significant way and will just waste their time and mine. I am learning to get out of God's way in another's life, yet be willing to do whatever He desires me to do for another.

Now I am more careful about what family, church, and societal laws I heed. Now I ask God about the practices and obligations I have inadvertently followed and try to heed only those He gives me motivation to engage in.

I am not willing to separate myself from the LORD to do my "good works." Living grace from within is too important a blessing to lose in order to look good to others.

My Life No Longer a Response

The first words I ever heard from the Lord were "don't let your life become a response." I knew it was the Lord speaking because it had such a transforming effect on me. I have never forgotten it. It surely wasn't something I was thinking or asking about. I knew immediately what He meant but I had no idea how profound this simple phrase would be in my life.

12

I hadn't realized just how much of my life had been a response to stimulus from without and how much this consumed my time and energy. I didn't listen within to my heart because I had been taught it was deceitful. My whole life was looking for guidance and direction from without.

I had been indoctrinated with don't be selfish, which meant that my desires came behind other's wishes. I had been taught to give my life away to and for others.

Initially I took God's words to mean that I wasn't to give myself away to others as readily as I had been. Eventually, I came to understand the seriousness of my approach to life. I was ignoring the Spirit of God within me and discounting the work of Christ.

How can God lead me and guide me if I refuse to listen and obey? How can He save me if I am not heeding His voice and promptings?

I was still trying to save myself. I was separating myself from God and therefore not experiencing His life. I was still in the world and of it because I was following the world's wisdom and understanding. I was still very much a people pleaser.

I wasn't a believer. I didn't believe in a LIVING SAVIOR or LIVING LORD. With His first words, the Lord introduced Himself to me and His desire to be LORD and SAVIOR of my life. *I had to learn to live from the inside out rather than from the outside in.*

I'd like to say I learned this lesson easily but it took years until I understood what He wanted from me. My desire to please Him was a continual hindrance to my resting in His presence within. I was intent on doing something for Him when He wanted my life.

Grace, as His divine influence upon my heart and His expression in and through me, is another step in affirming His first words to me.

13

Leading Versus Controlling

When we live under grace we must become leaders rather than followers of man. In order to follow God's Spirit we must listen within to God and follow His words. *To follow God's words within is to LEAD.* To heed man's words from without is to follow man.

Leading is not the same as controlling others. Leading is expressing God within. Leading is God's Spirit expressed through us, from the inside out. I lead as I follow the Leader within, my LORD. Others have the choice to receive, accept, and follow or not. I lead as God motivates me to will and to do of His good pleasure rather than responding to please others. I must live my own life which others have the choice to be part of or not.

Control, on the other hand, is using a position of authority or laws to demand, force, or punish another for not doing what I want, for example, a manager over an employee or parent over a child. Controllers want others to conform to their will. When people control us, we don't feel we have a choice to disagree without losing something—our job, our parent's love and acceptance, or acceptance in the church. We are not free to be who we are or to do what God is motivating in us. We are not free to live our own life.

God is teaching me the difference between leading and controlling. To lead I must:

1. Live my life.

    I must live what God motivates in me. God is asking me to let Him do His works through me for His glory not for me to do my works for my glory. I will answer for my life, not for others.

2. Share my life.

   I must have a life to share. Jesus said, "I am Life." He is the Tree of Life. I am to be a *witness* of Christ in me, that is, God working in and through me.

3. Give my life to God only

   I am to give my life to God only. I am to die to self and love God with my all. I am not my own anymore. I am dead so the Spirit of God in me can lead. I am not to give away my life to others like I have been. Instead of trying to please others and trying to belong to them, I am to belong to my LORD. Jesus did the sacrifice for everyone. Jesus is the Savior, not me.

4. Lead as God directs from within

   God wants all His children to lead so He can express Himself through each of us. God wants us to please Him, not man. We walk like Jesus. Jesus did only what the Father told Him to do. To follow the LORD in us is to live from the inside out rather than from the outside in. We are not to control or take authority over others. All are equal in the Body of Christ. My sisters and brothers are those who hear and do the will of God, that is, those who also lead following God within.

5. Stop looking for outside leadership to follow

   I am not to look to others to hear God's direction for my life. The Israelites wanted Moses to hear for them (Exodus 20:19). Then they wanted a king to lead them (1 Samuel 8:4-7). God was very upset with them in both instances. He warned them, but they insisted on having intermediaries between them and God. God wants direct communication with all His children.

My choice is to surrender and love God with all my heart. God can then do His work in and through me. I allow Him to lead through me. I live inside out. I live the life He motivates in me. I give my life to Him and please Him rather than giving my life to others and pleasing man. I do only what He motivates in me versus doing my good works.

Leading to Test the Spirit of Others

Another reason for leading is that by following God's Spirit within I automatically *test the spirit* of others.

When I lead from within, God's Spirit in me leads and others respond or react to God's Spirit just as they responded to or reacted to God's Spirit in Jesus, God's first son. *We discern the Spirit in others by their reaction to God's Spirit in us.* This is one way to test someone's spirit.

The religious leaders—Pharisees, Scribes, and Sadducees— reacted to Christ's Spirit—the Spirit of God in Him. Those not of God will not follow God's Spirit in us because they serve Satan, law, and the Tree of Knowledge of Good and Evil.

It is law or grace, but not both. We are either under the divine influence of God, with God's Spirit in us as our righteousness, or we are doing our own self-righteous works.

We can lead together if we are both of God:

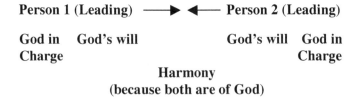

Person 1 (Leading) ⟶ ◀— **Person 2 (Leading)**

| **God in Charge** | **God's will** | | **God's will** | **God in Charge** |

Harmony
(because both are of God)

This doesn't mean these two will be exactly alike, but they will be expressing God individually and God is not in conflict with Himself.

If the spirit in two people is different, there is conflict. It becomes a spiritual battle because Satan works in and through those who are not of God. Therefore, in a relationship if one is of God and the other is not of God there will be conflict.

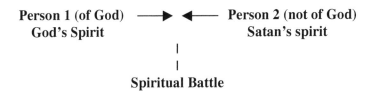

Person 1 (of God) ⟶ ⟵ **Person 2 (not of God)**
God's Spirit   **Satan's spirit**

Spiritual Battle

The one not of God will not follow the one of God because Satan in them will not follow God's Spirit. The one of God cannot follow the one not of God or they will end up following Satan.

I have found that in order to make peace with those not of God I must SIN and separate from God. When I try to be at peace with them I am forced to override my heart and as a consequence be deceitful. I SIN and Satan gets control of my life by my trying to please others.

When I made my commitment to listen and obey the Lord, my relationship with some individuals was negatively affected. This came as both a surprise and sorrow. When the Spirit of God within has opportunity to manifest, others react to the Spirit of God in us. Even though my light is a flickering wick, those who have given Satan control in their life reject even this small expression of His presence in me. It feels like rejection of me and often is. This I have come to understand is suffering for Christ's sake. Often the other person doesn't realize what happened in our relationship. Many of us are unaware of this aspect of the spiritual dimension even though the Bible clearly explains it.

Those who refuse to submit to the LORD but desire this world and its pleasures, are convicted by God's Spirit in us whether we are aware of it or not. At first, this brought great sorrow and confusion into my life trying to figure out what happened in these relationships.

God's Spirit within has faithfully explained what happened in the spiritual realm. In the earthly realm nothing made sense and I spent weeks, months, and even years trying to understand what went wrong in a relationship when there is no answer except in the spiritual realm. I have learned to ask God to explain what occurred rather than trying to figure out what went wrong. I am a slow learner but this lesson has been a big one for me and I pray I will not forget it.

One early example of this occurred when I was getting my Masters degree. I was sitting in class one day when a man came up to me and accused me of not liking him. I was totally taken aback because I hadn't even thought about him. This puzzled me for a long time and I wondered what I had done to make this man feel unaccepted by me.

It wasn't until many years later that I ran into a classmate who told me what this man had been doing. Apparently, he had some major involvement in prostitution and extra marital affairs. According to her, others knew it but I was totally unaware. The only way I can explain this incident is that his darkness was so great that my little light could be seen. It was not that I was so spiritual, but that his darkness was very great.

Since then I have found that those who look good on the outside, but have not given themselves to the LORD, will also react in negative and strange ways toward me. Just as in Christ's day, when the religious people reacted to Him, so these same folk will react to me when God's Spirit is manifested in and through me.

God's Spirit convicts just by His presence without us doing anything in particular. I have found myself saying something that I had not premeditated that seems to really irritate another person. On the surface, I cannot explain their reaction, because what I said has no apparent bearing on their life. When I see their reaction, I have come to believe that there has been conviction by the Spirit.

One of the hardest tests of my faith has been when God lets me see the spirit in another person. I have always believed the best about another person and others have to do something pretty awful to me for me to not like or trust them. I thought this was a good quality. I am learning to trust God's Spirit in me and heed His revelation about the spirit in others.

I am not yet mature in seeing the spirit of another, but God is teaching me. He sees and saves me from the hidden motivations of others. As a good parent He lets me learn the hard way by trusting someone I shouldn't, then shows me that He warned me but I did not listen.

Have you ever questioned someone's sincerity and then chastised yourself for judging them when you really have no facts to substantiate your distrust, you just have an intuition?

When God taught me the difference between judging another based on the law and testing the spirit of another, I was surprised to learn that *my beliefs were interfering with my believing*. I overruled Christ within who was showing me that God's Spirit within me was not in harmony with the spirit of the other. Instead of listening, I was clinging to the verses that said I was not to judge others. I questioned His words to me because it violated one of my beliefs.

I am learning not to violate my own heart and thus deny Christ in me. I have come to believe God's words to me and the motivations He puts on my heart. Faith comes by hearing the words of God.

Resolved to Live From My Heart—No Deceit

As Christians, we want to love and give, but in so doing we often slip into the enemy's territory of deceit. We do things for others, which do not reflect our heart. Although we don't want to do it, we feel that we should if we are good Christians.

We have all kinds of excuses for living a lie. I know because I have used them.

> **I don't want to** hurt someone's feelings so I get together with them when they ask, even though my heart isn't in it.

> **I should** do a certain task because I want unbelievers to see God's love in me. How else are they going to know the love of God if I don't do this?

> **I have to** contribute to church programs, so I will do my part even though I don't want to.

> I **have to** attend church or this event to be a "good" example to those around me.

> **I will do what this person wants** because I don't want to be selfish.

I felt good about myself for doing "good works" until the Lord showed me that when I live a lie I give Satan, the father of lies, an opening into my life. This is not a small thing because Satan uses every opening to get a greater grip on our life.

Often this occurs because we live out of our mind and belief systems. It is our mind that comes up with "good works" and gets us to SIN and ignore the Spirit of God in our heart. Our mind likes to control our heart and we've been taught to have our mind rule our heart. But this mind control is just another way of taking control back from the Spirit of God in our heart. Mind censoring is law, not grace.

Have you ever experienced how one small deception creates situations requiring additional deceit? When I support an activity where my heart is not engaged, this always produces another engagement that I feel obligated to attend. When I show feigned attention toward someone, it produces another invitation that I feel obligated to accept. Satan always takes more ground when I live a little white lie.

When Jesus said we receive the Spirit of Truth, He meant just that. The Spirit of Truth, God's Spirit within us, doesn't motivate us to live a lie or be deceitful. Therefore, when we engage in these practices we open ourselves up to Satan and his spirit within.

The Lord showed me clearly that He didn't accept any of my excuses for living anything less than absolute truth. He is TRUTH and when I live TRUTH I live in Him. I was surprised at how adamant the Lord is about this. I have come to realize that any deceit endangers not only my own life but also the life of those I engage in my deceit.

For example, when I deceitfully flatter another, I live in deceit and the other person also becomes part of my lie. They can take what I said and live their life believing this lie is true. Lies produce more lies. Truth produces more truth. Lies put everyone in bondage. Truth sets us free.

When I am less than honest with another, afterwards I feel unsettled and disheartened. This is a reminder of what confusion and turmoil the enemy can inject into my life with deceit.

In classes I showed a film that illustrated the effect of agreeing with others just to create harmony. The scene is the living room where a family is gathered. One person suggests going to get some ice cream. Another person, wanting to cooperate, says she would like to go for ice cream too, even though she really doesn't want to. Then another person says he wants to go so as not to disappoint the two who just said they wanted to go.

Eventually they all agree to go for ice cream even though no one really wants to go. The film goes on to show the miserable time they have as they execute this agreed-to plan. Finally, at the end you see one of them confess that he really didn't want to go but did so for the sake of the others. Each person in turn reveals that he or she did not want to go either. The person who suggested it even admits that he did not want to go. So they all went where none of them wanted to go.

How often does this happen in families and church organizations where a member lives a lie supposedly to support some other member? I see it happen. We show up because others expect our attendance. We feel forced to contribute so we choose to please man and disregard God's Spirit.

Therefore, I am committed to listen to God's Spirit in my heart and to live consistent with my heart motivations. If I truly believe that God's Spirit resides in my heart and is the source of TRUTH, then I must not violate my own heart. Anything else is living a lie.

What is the worst that can happen if I follow my heart? I expose the enemy's occupancy. This is good, because then I can repent and turn around before He gets a grip that is harder to loosen. Why would I conceal my heart and who the occupant is?

To remind myself not to be deceitful, I keep the following phrase on my desk:

HEART = WORDS & ACTIONS

There is no excuse in God's eyes for stretching the truth and telling a lie. Satan is the father of lies and he is our father when we live a lie or are deceitful in anything we do.

We justify our actions with many excuses and then wonder why we don't hear God's voice or feel loved by Father God. We don't realize that we have left Him and need to repent.

Grace is God's Spirit expressed through us. How could we ever attribute lies to the Spirit of Truth?

No More Self-Analysis

When we give our life to the Lord, we don't seem to realize that it is no longer ours. When we present our bodies to Him, He proceeds to cleanse the vessel. He does the work in us. Our responsibility and work is to *believe in Him* to do the work in and through us.

One indication of whether I believe the LORD is in charge of my life is the amount of self-analysis I engage in. I have a habit of analyzing my thoughts, words, and actions in a critical manner. I often do a replay of what has occurred and begin analyzing if what I see is good or bad. I am especially prone to engage in this if other's reactions to me are not positive. I go through the "shoulds" and "wish I hads." I proceed to the I wish I wasn't this or that. The LORD has shown me that this conduct is the result of me still thinking that I am in charge and responsible. He has shown me that I separate myself from Him by this behavior.

Do you ever take stock of your spiritual life to see if you are living as a Christian? Some of us do this more consciously than others do, but we all do it to some degree. If we are satisfied with our spiritual life, it is probably because we subconsciously or consciously have a set of criteria we think we are meeting. I go to church every Sunday, I am an elder, I tithe, and I support several programs at the church. We all have our criteria.

Often our more conscious self-analysis occurs when someone questions our faith or when some situation we thought was of God doesn't turn out the way we expected. We examine our own behavior and try to justify it or take stock and resolve to correct our conduct. When something doesn't go according to our plan, we question our ability to hear God and fear making additional mistakes.

In God's view, this self-analysis is of the enemy. Yes, of the enemy! I didn't accept this the first time the Lord pointed it out to me.

The way God explained it to me was life changing. He showed me that if I really believed in Him then I believed that His Spirit was in me and active. If I have surrendered to God, His Spirit in me expresses Himself in and through me. It is His work, not mine. My only job is to *believe in Him*.

If I am going to self-analyze, it should be limited to assessing if I am believing in Him. Have I made Him LORD of my life? Did I submit to Him or not?

I am not to concentrate on the sins but on the SIN, which is separation from God. Are we one or not? Did I mean it when I gave Him my life or not? This I can answer because I know if I meant it or not. Do I need to repent or not?

Questions about the reactions of others to us or to question situations we find ourselves in only leads us into assessing beliefs, and the laws we create from them. It leads us down the path to self-control and away from God's Spirit within.

The LORD showed me that I don't get better, He is the source of all my GOOD. Without Him I have no goodness and whatever happens occurs because of oneness with Him or my separation from Him.

My work is to believe in Him and this means to stay in union with Him. When I do this He is in charge and it is His work that I am experiencing and not my own. Whatever He does is GOOD. If it is bad, it is only because I have separated myself from Him.

The LORD is teaching me to come to Him with my questions to see what He did in the situation rather than analyzing my own actions as coming only from me. In this way, I have learned some great lessons on how to live my life in Christ. This gives my LORD the opportunity to help me unlearn many lessons learned in order to control my life. He desires to be my GOD, my only God.

I can ask Him to explain what happened, but I am not to go down the self-recrimination path or the poor-me road. I have a simple choice to make. Do I *believe* God's Spirit is in me and in charge or don't I? If I question it, my work is to *repent* and reaffirm my commitment.

Self-analysis is an indication that we are separated from God. How else could we feel responsible for the words and actions we are analyzing?

The LORD showed me this when I was in one of my down-on-myself times. I was analyzing my lack of progress in my faith and how I felt so inadequate to be the person I felt He wanted me to be. His question to me was: Have you asked me to be LORD of your life? To this I could honestly answer in the affirmative. Then He asked me if I believed that He did come and was in charge? When He asked this I knew I was in trouble because if I questioned His coming I knew I was disparaging His character. He promises to come if we choose to give Him our life. I answered that I did believe He came and that I wanted Him to be in charge. His next question riveted into my unbelief and discouragement. He asked: If I am in charge, who is responsible for your growth and actions? I thought this was a trick question because all I could answer is that responsibility lies with the one in charge. Then I was humbled by His next question: If I am in charge and responsible, would you judge Me? And what law would you use to judge Me? This marked the end of our discussion and the beginning of my *repentance*.

After this discussion, I saw this Scripture which I believe captures what the Lord was teaching me about self-analysis.

The spiritual man judges all things, but is himself to be **judged by no one.** *"For who has known the mind of the*

Lord so as to instruct him?" But we have the mind of
Christ.   *1 Corinthians 2:15-16*

When I give the Lord my life, I am to be judged by no one, including myself.

When I judge myself, I use the laws of good and evil. If I try to keep one law, I am bound to keep the whole law and I fall from grace.

I testify again to every man who receives circumcision [obeys this one law] *that he is bound to keep the whole law.* **You are severed from Christ, you who would be justified by the law; you have fallen away from grace.**
                                       Galatians 5:3-4

When we ask God to be LORD, He comes and fulfills this role. Only we can separate ourselves from Him. He doesn't leave us, we leave Him with our own willfulness and pride. I need to remind myself everyday that He is my Life and the source of any GOOD that may be done in and through me.

I am learning to come to the LORD and ask Him to explain what is happening in my life. I find that He is very willing to explain what I need to know. He knows what I need to understand. Often, He takes me through new experiences to show me what happened in a previous situation.

We have a Father who is very willing to work in and through us when we make the choice to have Him be the divine influence upon our heart. This is living grace. All else is living under law.

No More Testing God or Claiming Scripture

Another pitfall is my tendency to want God to act according to what I read in Scripture. If He says He is the healer, I want to see Him heal me and others. If He says He protects His children, I want to see that He does because I don't like to see His children suffer.

I used to consider asking God to fulfill a Bible verse as an act of faith. The Lord has shown me otherwise.

He reminds me periodically that I am to believe in Him and not in words He spoke to others in the past. He is a Living LORD and SAVIOR. He speaks today and expects me to obey His words and not claim Bible verses.

He pointed out that I wouldn't want the people who reported to me 20 years ago to still be carrying out my management directives today. I had to agree with that.

The Bible was written to bring us to Christ and to the Father, not to replace them. I hadn't realized that I was using the Bible to get to know about God and then using what was said to make God obey me. That is exactly what we do when we claim Scripture. We put God to the test. We call on Him to prove Himself by obeying words He said or someone recorded generations ago. Satan quoted Scripture to get Jesus to test God and he tries to get us to do the same. Jesus responded by saying He listens to God the Father and does only what the Father is telling Him to do— He did not put God to the test by claiming Scripture.

The Israelites tested God in the wilderness and suffered the consequences of not entering the promised land.

The Lord's directive to me is to listen and obey Him. He is the same today, yesterday and forever. He wants His children to obey "today, when they hear His voice." The Bible and the laws were put in place to bring us to Him so we can hear Him.

Knowing the Lord does not come by reading the Bible or by reading about other people's experiences of faith. Knowing the Lord comes from experiencing Him in and through us. It is our oneness with the Lord that allows us to *know* Him. Knowing

God is very different from knowledge *about* Him or having Bible knowledge.

The obedience God is asking of us is not obedience of Scripture, but obedience to His voice today. He is a person, not a set of written words.

Living in grace is heeding the voice of God's Spirit from within—His divine influence on my heart.

Lessening of My Looking to Worldly Authorities

Once we hear the voice of God from within there is less need to depend on authorities from without.

Was it the educated Pharisees and Scribes that Jesus chose as disciples or the uneducated fishermen who were willing to follow Him? Is it the educated Bible scholar of today that Jesus would choose or the simple laborer who listens to Him?

Much of man's authority is derived from education and positions of power and wealth, not from God's authority from within. Most of the authority structures are put in place to control man and keep order. With God in control, He is my ultimate authority and much more effective than laws or man's authority.

Man's knowledge is often incomplete and inaccurate. How often have we seen what was once considered good later be deemed as bad. Consider nutrition or medical practices. One day we are to eat eggs and butter, the next they are considered bad, then they are good for us again. Taking certain drugs are good for us one day and then we find out they are harmful.

Instead of depending on man's knowledge and wisdom, I now try to depend on God's leading from within. Do I go to a doctor or do I wait to see if God wants to heal me? Do I go to this class or do I let God teach me. Now I depend on God's leading more and less on my mind, knowledge, or going to experts and authorities.

Mind knowledge puffs up and mind-educated authorities like doctors, professors and Bible scholars think they know when they do not know. Most of these educated experts don't recognize God as the only one who truly knows.

Many of these so-called experts and authorities are not listening to God and are too proud to consider submitting to Him. Therefore, I have come to question why I would listen to the voice of Satan through them. If they are not of God, then they are of Satan and speak the words of the master liar.

While I am not weaned from this completely, I have come a long way in guarding what I pick up as good from worldly experts.

Wisdom comes from the Lord. Living grace—under God's divine influence—is wisdom.

Stop Studying Evil to Avoid Evil and Be Good

The avoidance of evil does not make us good. God is GOOD and only what He does in and through us is good.

My attempts to understand evil only gives Satan opportunity to plant his words in my mind and subsequently to get me to fear evil. I realize now that my attempts to avoid evil cause me to take back control from God, separating myself from Him.

When I read newspapers or watch TV programs about robberies, murders, and other evils I find that these pollute my mind and create fears. Constantly watching these evils numbs me to wickedness like a frog in a slowly heated pot. Divorce and deceptive business practices become so common I begin to accept them as inevitable. I no longer allow God to show me His perspective.

Why do we think we need to know about evil to avoid it? If we have truly given our life to the LORD, He isn't going to lead us into evil. I need to trust the LORD in me to guard and rescue me from all evils.

*The Lord is faithful; he will strengthen you and **guard you from evil.*** *2 Thessalonians 3:3*

The Lord will rescue me from every evil *and save me for his heavenly kingdom.* *2 Timothy 4:18*

When I feel like I need to protect myself, it's a clue that I am in fear and trying to avoid evil. I have most likely taken back control of my life.

God can motivate us in a way that we avoid evil without even being aware of it. He can motivate us to drive a certain route that keeps us from an accident. He can keep us from going to a dishonest person by motivating us to go to another. He is committed to protecting us, His children.

We often don't realize that we are like Eve in the Garden of Eden when she took of the Tree of the Knowledge of Good and Evil. She already knew GOOD because God is GOOD and everything He created was good. What she gained by eating of the tree was to know evil so she could decide between good and evil. We do this when we study Scripture to know good and evil. God is GOOD. Even Jesus said He wasn't good, only God the Father was good. So we need not know good and evil, we need only to listen to GOOD, which is listening and obeying God's voice within.

You might ask then, why bad things happen to believers. God allows what we consider bad to bring us closer to Him. Some of the losses I have experienced, where it felt like God wasn't taking care of me, have turned out to be blessings in disguise. I sure would never have orchestrated the circumstances or the results, but in hindsight I see how it brought me closer to the LORD and away from situations that were not good for me. God turns everything into good when we trust Him and let Him do His work in and through us.

We know that in everything God works for good with those who love him, who are called according to his purpose.   *Romans 8:28*

Living in grace is GOOD and avoiding evil.

Resolved to Look Like a Fool

I have come to realize that I cannot hold on to my reputation if I am committed to following the Lord. God's ways are so different from the world's.

People of the world will never understand what God is motivating in and doing through me. Most will judge me as a fool for the decisions I make.

This was hard for me to accept at first. It is especially hard for some of us who cherish reputation in our family and church. Once I gave the Lord my life, I realized I am playing to an audience of one—God alone. This made looking like a fool easier to accept.

God changes us when we give Him our life. Where once making money was our goal, we now are willing to accept we have enough. How many people have you heard say they are content with the amount of money they have? God can do this in our life and it does not play well to a worldly audience.

How many of those who desire reputation and advantage are willing to side with the underdog when others they wish to please do not?

Those who want to be somebody in this world are rarely willing to be a nobody, yet alone look like a fool. This is especially difficult for those who value a good reputation.

As I walk the path of grace, I have seen my values change and become quite different from my former worldly values. Reputation with others has lessoned its grip on me. Following the traditions and customs of certain organizations no longer has such a hold on me. I have a long way to go, but I can sense these laws and authorities have less affect on me.

When I start analyzing how I spend my time and mistakenly use worldly values to assess it, I begin to wonder if I am a fool to give up so much to follow the Lord. When I am with others who try to live both in God's kingdom and in the world, I see myself not measuring up to my old standards of success.

Coming out of the world to follow the Lord will make you feel like an outsider in many of the environments where you formerly felt comfortable and accepted. There will be times when you question your own decision to be of God and leave the world's ways.

All I can do is to encourage you to hold on to the Lord and ride it out. I know that I need other believers to affirm my walk. God has graciously provided this encouragement when He knew I needed it. I am fortunate that my husband and I are on the same path so we can encourage each other. We need the fellowship of other believers.

Most important, however, is to focus on our walk of grace and not try be part of the world. We cannot be of God and of the world. Other so-called Christians who do this are a detriment to my walk. I am learning to be careful what I pick up from people who speak like believers, but their conduct is no different from that of the world.

One writer that I admire said that if your life is the same as before you committed your life to the Lord, you really haven't made God Lord of your life. He goes on to say that the only evidence of a true commitment are the losses in your life. I have found this to be true. God is faithful when we give Him our life, He goes to work purging out the dross.

Living grace exposes and roots out our worldly life. What is left makes us look like fools to those of the world. When I have felt this way and cried out to the Lord, He said, "A fool to whom?" Then, He encourages me, "You are not a fool in my eyes."

I have had to resolve to be a fool for the LORD.

Fear Is Satan's Motivator to Get Control of Us

How easy it is to take back control from God. I recognize now that fear often is the main trigger for me taking back control and separating myself from God's divine influence. Fear shows up in many forms: fear of failure, fear of rejection by others, fear of illness, and the list goes on.

God gave me choice to believe in Him and obey His voice and leading or to go it alone with my intellect and knowledge.

How quickly I fall into the grip of fear as I rely on my mind. My instinct is to want to understand any situation that has caused fear, which is usually some form of evil. It is either a person being a messenger of Satan or a situation that is evil. Once I start down the road of trying to understand evil, my fear grows and my instinct to take control increases.

I still need to learn the lesson of not dwelling on evil—not even receiving it because I find myself at the Tree of Knowledge of Good and Evil and separate from God. He doesn't separate from me; I separate from Him. I still fall into the trap of thinking I can avoid evil by understanding it. This is a lie.

The LORD gave me a diagram that helped me see the insidiousness of trying to understand evil and how it leads me away from the *living* God within me. This chart clearly shows the choice we have of where we focus our attention and the results of our choices. *Good is the opposite of evil yet we don't get to good by eliminating evil. Evil is the nature and work of the devil. Good is the nature and work of God.* God and the devil are infinitely far from each other. We are either looking at one or the other but not both. The choice of our focus and attention is ours to make and fear or faith are the outcome.

My fears are a warning to change my focus. When I fear I realize that Satan has my attention and I need to turn around and repent. Whether the fear is God letting me know that all is not well or it's the enemy trying to lure me into understanding evil, I know now to repent and return my attention to God.

We have the choice of being at the Tree of the Knowledge of Good and Evil trying to be good and avoid evil or of having God, who is GOOD, in charge of our life. God in me is the Tree of Life. Relying on and following God, who is GOOD, results in good.

Only God in charge of my life can make me be and do good.

Jesus didn't claim to be good and insisted that only God the Father was good. Christ's goodness came from God the Father reigning in and through Him. He did nothing but what the Father said or did through Him.

Jesus is our role model.

Chapter 2: Living Grace: My Heart Relationship With God My Father

God influences our life from His throne within our heart when we give Him our life.

Grace Is a Heart Relationship With God Our Father

God isn't interested in controlling our life. He desires this influence on our heart so that we know Him and have an intimate relationship with Him.

God wants a relationship with us like He had with His only begotten Son, Jesus. Jesus loved the Father and did nothing but what the Father said and did. God, our Father, desires to have this same oneness with us and this requires that He have the same influence upon our heart.

God created us for relationship with Him. We see this in the Garden of Eden before Adam and Eve decided to disobey.

Relationships are a function of the heart so God chooses to influence our heart and reign there. If He just desired to control us, He could do that through our mind, but He chose the heart.

The way I establish relationship with God my Father is to acknowledge His residence in my heart by listening to my heart, obeying the words He speaks to me, and by heeding the promptings of my heart.

In other words, I believe that He sent His Spirit into my heart, as Scripture attests, and act on it. I *believe in Him* by living as Jesus did in oneness with the Father and said we too are one with God the Father through Him.

Relationship with God is a oneness relationship where we are in union with Him. It isn't a forced relationship. I always have choice to give Him access to my life or not. It is a love relationship by choice.

At first, this walk in God's Spirit can be scary. To submit to another is frightening especially when we are not sure we trust the other. That is why it is so important to know God the Father. Most of us think we know Him but we really only know about Him. We read Scripture and think we know God. Yet what person would say they know another person by just reading their autobiography or biography. We know how they conducted themselves with others but we don't know a person until we are with them and know them at a heart level.

For me the key is to believe that I am one with God's Spirit, and to live as if this is true. I listen to His voice and promptings in my heart and obey. This is faith and living in grace.

LOVE Is My Focus

The Lord has shown me clearly that there is no definition of love except GOD IS LOVE. Love isn't something I do, but God flowing in and through me. He is the only love I have to give.

Therefore, I seek to listen to LOVE in my heart and do only what He shows me to do. I see His love for me this way and I see His love for others this way.

I no longer define loving actions by my previous definitions because I realize that love is not what I thought it was. I used to think it was being "nice" and "loving" to others, which often meant I would give of myself to them. I accepted others and tried to encourage them. I spent some of my life's work helping people discover who they were and what they were to do with their life.

When the Lord showed me that He is LOVE and the only definition of love, I had to reexamine my "loving" actions. Was I only doing what He motivated me to do or was I doing works I thought was love? I came to see that these loving actions of mine were the 'good works' that Jesus detested as self-righteousness.

It took quite a while for the Lord to convince me that I could rely on His expression through me to be the love He was wanting from me for others.

He did this by emphasizing that the *first* commandment required me to love Him with my *all*. This in essence is allowing Him to be in charge of my life—His divine influence. He focused me here for a long time and I realize now why this had to be my first step of faith. I had to let God, who is LOVE, be in charge of my heart. Once He is, then I can let Him, LOVE, flow in me and through me.

His LOVE in my heart is the love I have been searching for my whole life. We all want to be loved. Only God, LOVE, can satisfy this hunger. Giving God my heart was the first time I truly felt loved. I don't know how I came to feel loved, it just was. LOVE is.

As I allow God to love through me, I am getting a new understanding of what love looks like. I am coming to understand more of how God has been working with me and how some of my suffering and pain were God's love. This sounds lofty, but became real as I allowed God to be LOVE in my heart. I can see now how some of the suffering and pain others experience is really God's love wooing them to Himself. My old concept of love of trying to alleviate their pain, is not LOVE.

Repent is my key for giving God divine influence in my life; LOVE is my key for giving God access to my heart.

Living in grace lifts the burden of trying to love God and others and opens up an exciting adventure of seeing LOVE in action in my own life and His LOVE through me to others.

Hearing God's Spirit In My Heart

Because I ask God to be in charge of my life and make Him LORD, I can listen to my heart. God comes when He is invited. God's Spirit comes and resides in my heart. My work is to believe that He comes and is reigning there.

To hear and follow I need to recognize God's divine influence upon my heart and allow Him expression in my life. I listen to my heart and believe that it is my LORD speaking to me. He speaks to me in a still small voice from within my heart.

I spend time in the morning writing out my prayers because God is speaking to me and I want to honor Him by recording His words. I always take notes when I am listening to some authority or expert. In college I took copious notes from my professors — some I still have in my library. I record my prayers because I am listening to my heavenly Father — the source of *all* truth.

What surprised me about writing while praying is that some of the extraneous thoughts I used to block out because I found them distracting, are in fact the Lord trying to change the subject. When I initiate a conversation about some troubling situation, the Lord often reminds me about some truth that I need to understand first. I often hear Christians say their mind wanders when they pray. I wonder if God is trying to speak to them and they attribute it to a distraction like I did for many years. Don't get me wrong, there can be distractions, but when you write your prayers and let your heart speak, you will discover like I did that most often the Lord is trying to redirect our conversation to deal with the underlying issue.

Jesus said:

He who believes in me, as the scripture has said, 'Out of his heart shall flow rivers of living water.' Now this he said about the Spirit, which those who believed in him were to receive; for as yet the Spirit had not been given, because Jesus was not yet glorified.   *John 7:38-39*

God puts His Spirit in my heart and it is His Spirit that speaks to me. His words from my heart are the living water that Jesus speaks of here. When we speak forth these words, they are living waters to the hearer.

We are warned repeatedly about an *unbelieving heart* because God reigns in our heart. He speaks and motivates us to do His will from His throne there. When we don't listen to our heart, we are in unbelief. If God says He puts His Spirit in our heart when we ask Him to, then we need to believe in Him and listen to our heart. God gives us a new redeemed heart when He becomes the occupant. God is alive and He lives within your heart and mine. Our heart is where we choose to believe or not.

By communicating with God my Father and Jesus I get to know them intimately. How else do we get to know another? Without two-way communication, I would not have a relationship with another person. So how can I expect to know God without communing with Him? This is not just listening and obeying orders, but a dialogue between me and my Father. I ask questions and God willingly teaches me what I need to know.

God is not interested in giving commands that we hear and obey. He is interested in developing a love relationship with us. This has been the result for me by communing with my LORD. How can you not love someone when He gives you His life? How can you not love this Father who patiently teaches and explains all things to you? Listening to God within our heart is all about relationship. You will find, as I did, that He is far more interested in relationship than He is in having you work for Him or issuing commands.

Jesus could honestly say that God's commands are not burdensome. This is true. Our thinking that God is going to give us some distasteful assignment is a lie of the enemy. Whatever God asks you to do, He does it through you. He does it all, He just needs our cooperation. Most of the things He asks of me are learning experiences for both me and another. As He works through me, I get to know Him better and our relationship deepens.

Jesus' disciples were always asking Him to explain what was happening or what a parable meant. Jesus patiently explained parables and taught them. God's Spirit in us teaches us *all* things if we will listen.

I have been amazed at what the Lord teaches me—everything from the effects of antibiotics on B vitamins to the widespread detrimental use of prescribed drugs. He knows all and is willing to teach us all things.

One advantage of writing my prayers and conversations with God my Father is that I can reread them and in hindsight see what He has been teaching me and how He led me. Often when I reread these writings I gain further insights as the eyes of my heart are opened to His presence and working in me.

I strongly recommend writing your prayers and rereading them. Write to learn. Tell God your concerns and record what He says to you. This will be a blessing beyond description. My morning writings continue to build up my faith in my LIVING LORD and keep me from returning to law and the world.

Many Christians, including myself, are content to read the Bible and have one-way prayers with God the Father. It wasn't until I realized that God talked one-on-one with people in the Bible that I began to open up to the possibility of Him talking with me.

Once I believed that He might want to talk with me, I sought to hear Him speak to me in my prayer time. When He spoke, it resonated in my heart and I felt it changed me. Faith came when I believed and acted on what He was saying.

Many Christians are afraid to hear God's voice. Some believe that the Bible has replaced God speaking today. This I find incredulous. Why would a LIVING FATHER have His words written down and then stop talking to His children? The Bible surely does not teach this for God spoke to people throughout the Bible. Jesus came and spoke man to man. God is more interested in having His voice heard than in reading His written word. Consider the following Scriptures. They have been instrumental in helping me have faith to listen to God's voice coming from within my heart. I pray that they will help you believe in your LIVING LORD within.

If you obey the voice of the LORD your God, being careful to do all his commandments which I command you this day, the LORD your God will set you high above all the nations of the earth. And all these blessings shall come upon you and overtake you, if you obey the voice of the LORD your God...."But if you will not obey the voice of the LORD your God or be careful to do all his commandments and his statutes which I command you this day, then all these curses shall come upon you and overtake you.... All these curses shall come upon you and pursue you and overtake you, till you are destroyed, because you did not obey the voice of the LORD your God, to keep his commandments and his statutes which he commanded you."

Deuteronomy 28:1-2,15, 45

Therefore, as the Holy Spirit says, "Today, when you hear his voice, do not harden your hearts as in the rebellion, on the day of testing in the wilderness, where your fathers put me to the test and saw my works for forty years. Therefore I was provoked with that generation, and said, 'They always go astray in their hearts; they have not known my ways.' As I swore in my wrath, 'They shall never enter my rest.'" **Take care, brethren, lest there be in any of you an evil, unbelieving heart, leading you to fall away from the living God.** *But exhort one another every day, as long as it is called "**today**," that none of you may be hardened by the deceitfulness of sin. For we share in Christ, if only we hold our first confidence firm to the end, while it is said,* **"Today, when you hear his voice, do not harden your hearts** *as in the rebellion." Hebrews 3:7-15*

Since therefore it remains for some to enter it, and those who formerly received the good news failed to enter because of disobedience, again he sets a certain day, **"Today,"** *saying through David so long afterward, in the words already quoted,* **"Today, when you hear his voice, do not harden your hearts."** *Hebrews 4:6-7*

Entering into a two-way conversation with God my Father and Jesus is a blessing beyond words. This no man shall take from me. Faith comes by hearing the word of God. He is the WORD. And His WORD is LIFE.

So then faith cometh by hearing, and hearing by the word of God. *Romans 10:17 (KJV)*

This is the active, present tense word of God—the *rhema*. The same word is used when Jesus rebuked Satan with, *"It is written, 'Man shall not live by bread alone,* **but by every word** *[rhema]* **that proceeds from the mouth of God.'"**

Hearing God's voice is a result of living in grace—heeding our LIVING LORD within speaking to us from our heart.

42

Following My Heart

Eventually I came to realize that I also had to trust that God's Spirit was motivating me to action and that it was not always going to be through words, but according to the *desires* He placed there.

Many situations don't allow for a written discussion of what the Lord desires from me because I have to live dynamically at the moment. I have to trust His Spirit in my heart to guide and lead me. Later, I can bring the situation to prayer and He can explain what I did not know or see at the time.

To be led by God's Spirit, I first believe that God's Spirit is in my heart and then follow my heart.

I write most mornings discussing with God the events of my life. He counsels me and assures me of His presence. Then I go about my day living from my heart. I follow my heart's desires because I believe they are God's will for me. I trust Him to motivate me to do His will.

I believe God when He says He motivates me to will and to do of His good pleasure.

> *God is at work in you, both to will and to work for his good pleasure.*   *Philippians 2:13*

I try to live such that my words and actions are sincere from my heart with no pretense.

HEART ➡ WORDS AND ACTIONS

If I am motivated in my heart to do something, I do it. If not, I don't. I can live this way because of my sincerity in asking God to be LORD of my life. I have a redeemed heart and this means God's Spirit is the occupant of my heart.

43

If I am not sincere about making God LORD of my life, then this kind of living is selfish and narcissistic. This would lead to all kinds of evil actions because Satan, the evil one, would be living out His words and actions through me.

God wants willing obedience that comes from a love relationship, not from deceitful acquiescence. In the Old Testament He motivated workers to build His tabernacle and to give generously.

To obey out of duty or fear is to do "good works" and to live a lie. I used to do things for others because I didn't want to be selfish. Now, I realize I was acting out of fear. Only words and actions from the heart are genuine and given willingly. God promises to motivate us to do His will.

Therefore, if I am doing anything inconsistent with my heart, I am in deceit and in the grip of Satan. Deceit in any form is a tool of the enemy and it makes no difference how good the work. Deceitful actions are the hallmark of "good works" that Jesus detested and Paul warned against.

Faith to heed His voice and follow the motivations He puts on my heart came by taking the first leap of faith and heeding His voice within and following His motivations in my heart. My faith gets stronger and less vulnerable each time I follow my heart and realize that my LORD is alive and living in me. This to me is *faith and believing in Him.*

Do I ever get frightened living like this? Yes, when I focus on others and their reactions. No, when I focus on my resident Lord and His word.

I trust my heart to know. As I walk through my day I do as He motivates me. This is my way of walking in His Spirit. Since He is Lord motivating me to will and to do of His will, I can trust that I am doing His will. I listen within and give credence to the words I hear in my heart. I let my heart rule over my mind, which is corrupted with beliefs that are not of God.

I am learning to trust, sometimes at some cost in reputation and acceptance by others. I know that this relationship is the pearl of great price and I pursue it as a priority. Like the man who went and sold all He had to buy the field where the pearl was found, I too desire to give up all to have this relationship.

Jesus lived this way. He did not follow others or give His life away to them. He gave His life to God and did His Father's will.

At some point, I had to step over the line and live in grace. I had to *believe* and *act* before I could experience God's presence in me.

How can my LORD save me if I don't heed His voice or follow the motivations He puts on my heart? How can I ever know His will and do it willingly unless He changes my heart to reflect His will?

God wants to lead us willingly from within. Faith is believing in Christ and how Jesus lived in relationship with God our Father. Jesus trusted God to work in and through Him.

Grace is following God's Spirit, the occupant of our heart. Grace is being led by God's Spirit within as Jesus was.

Heart Living Versus Mind Control

We believe with our heart and not our mind, so it is important to understand what it means to believe in our heart.

This means listening and obeying God's Spirit in my heart and heeding His promptings. Believing means I trust God with my life. I put Him in charge of my life.

My mind can store facts but it is not capable of relating to another. My mind can store beliefs, but I am not saved by my beliefs. I am saved by believing in my LIVING LORD within

45

me. *Beliefs in the mind result in religion; heart believing saves me.*

Believing and faith are not about obeying Scripture, but about relating to God our Father and Jesus. My heart is the place where I trust another or not. Therefore, I focus on believing in my heart and do so by following God's Spirit in my heart.

I try not to let my mind override my heart to make me socially acceptable and politically correct. My focus is on allowing God's Spirit within me to live in and through me. I try to allow Him to say what He wants to say and do what He wants to do without censorship from my mind.

I see two different ways that I follow the Lord within. One is to hear and heed what He speaks to me. The other way is to believe that He does motivate me to do His will so I can follow the motivations and desires of my heart. Again, I want to emphasize that this is all premised on the reality of me truthfully giving God my life and making Him the divine influence on my heart. The first step is to allow Him to be LORD. The next is to let Him express Himself in and through me. This is an act of *faith*— trusting my LIVING SAVIOR within.

Our FAITH begins with believing in our minds what God revealed about Himself in the Bible, but these beliefs must be put in action, that is, lived in our lives. Jesus died to save us and reconcile us to God our Father. He did it so that we can live as He lived. Jesus lived with God the Father as the Lord of His life. We too must not only say these words, but live with God reigning in us.

The enemy has been successful in getting us to fear listening to God's voice or heeding his promptings from within. If we don't listen to God's voice, we continue to live under the law, replacing the Old Testament law with New Testament verses. This is denial of Christ our LIVING SAVIOR.

My mind insists on having beliefs and laws to follow and, therefore, leads me back to works of the law. My heart, on the other hand, has the confidence to believe in a LIVING LORD within.

The Pure In Heart See God

When I commit to allowing the Lord to work in and through me, He can express Himself through me. When He does, I see Him. I see what He does through me and in me and I know that it is not me, but God.

A pure heart is a heart where God reigns. It is pure only because the one in charge is pure. Our prayer needs to be:

Create in me a clean heart, O God, and put a new and right spirit within me. Cast me not away from thy presence, and take not thy Holy Spirit from me.
Psalms 51:10-11

When Jesus said, "He who has seen me has seen the Father," He could say this because He was totally committed to doing only what Father God was doing and saying through Him. He manifested Father God to those around Him. Jesus and the Father were one.

You and I can manifest Father God to those around us by allowing God's Spirit to reign within us. God has provided all we need to abide in Him and obey His voice. Jesus died for us and won our reconciliation with our Father. We are sons and daughters of the LIVING God because God's Spirit is in charge of our life. We can have life as Jesus did if we *believe* in our LIVING LORD within and humbly allow Him to do His will in and through us. We see God when we live in grace.

Blessed are the pure in heart, for they shall see God.
Matthew 5:8

Living grace is seeing God as He expresses Himself in and through us.

Love for the Brethren

One wonderful result of allowing God's Spirit influence on my heart is my immediate love for my brethren.

When I find a believer who lives in grace, I immediately bond with them. It is because we are brothers and sisters, a family.

My spiritual family has become more important to me than my physical family. This is not to say that I don't value my physical family, but unless they too are living by the Spirit in grace, there is no bond of LOVE.

I enjoy being with those who have really committed themselves to the LORD because we encourage each other in our walk. There is an immediate identification with our experiences and struggles.

I had to learn that not all who call themselves Christian are my brothers and sisters. Some are wolves in sheep's clothing. Some are Satan's workers trying to keep me from believing and following my LORD.

Sometimes I'm surprised whom I relate to as a brother or sister considering differences in backgrounds and personalities. One woman, in particular, I consider a very dear sister in the LORD. We can share for hours about our walk and still desire more time together. When she reads my writings, she understands immediately and I can tell she has heard the same messages from the LORD.

There is an instant attraction and oneness of Spirit between true believers. Oneness in God's Spirit binds us together.

The apostle John addresses this *agape* love for the brethren:

*We love [agape], because he first loved [agape] us. If any one says, "I love [agape] God," and hates his brother, he is a liar; **for he who does not love [agape] his brother whom he has seen, cannot love [agape] God whom he has not seen**. And this commandment we have from him, that **he who loves [agape] God should love [agape] his brother also**.* 1 John 4:19-21

*By this it may be seen who are the children of God, and who are the children of the devil: whoever does not do right is not of God, **nor he who does not love [agape] his brother**. For this is the message which you have heard from the beginning, that **we should love [agape] one another**.... We know that we have passed out of death into life, **because we love [agape] the brethren**.... By this we know love [agape], that he laid down his life for us; and **we ought to lay down our lives for the brethren**.* 1 John 3:10-16

If we love God we will automatically love God's Spirit in our brothers and sisters in Christ. There is a oneness love bond between those who live in oneness with God's Spirit. We can lay down our lives for them, because in effect we are laying down our lives to God's Spirit in them.

Learning to Guard My Heart

In sharp contrast to love for the brethren is my heart response to those 'not of God'. I may want to relate to them and give to them but my heart becomes disheartened when I try to do so.

When I share my faith with those who call themselves Christian often nothing is received by them from me and nothing is received by me from them. Afterwards, my heart is disheartened.

It is as if we are on different wavelengths and so we are. Not all who call themselves Christians are believers.

The Lord has shown me that I am to discern the spirit of others before I open up my heart to receive from them. My tendency is receive another without discerning their spirit first. God has been working to show me the spiritual realm beneath what I see on the surface. Many so-called Christians are not of Him and I am not to receive from them. Satan, in these false Christians, uses my openness to speak to me and discourage me. God is teaching me to guard my heart when around those not of God, but I have been a slow learner.

God is love and always displays Himself as love in and through us. Therefore, I can always have my heart open to *give* LOVE, that is, let God flow in and through me, but I am not to be open to *receive* from others who have a different spirit. I am not to allow Satan's spirit in others to have any affect on me.

When Jesus said the following, He was talking about people who had God's Spirit in them. He calls them "my brethren."

*Then the King will say to those at his right hand, 'Come, O blessed of my Father, inherit the kingdom prepared for you from the foundation of the world; for **I was hungry and you gave me food, I was thirsty and you gave me drink, I was a stranger and you welcomed me, I was naked and you clothed me, I was sick and you visited me, I was in prison and you came to me.**' Then the righteous will answer him, 'Lord, when did we see thee hungry and feed thee, or thirsty and give thee drink? And when did we see thee a stranger and welcome thee, or naked and clothe thee? And when did we see thee sick or in prison and visit thee?' And the King will answer them, '**Truly, I say to you, as you did it to one of the least of these my brethren, you did it to me.**'* Matthew 25:34-40*

Jesus is not talking here about giving to the world at large. He is talking about giving to our brothers and sisters in God's family. Jesus refers to them as brethren—His brothers and sisters. Jesus is not in those who do not acknowledge Him and believe in Him.

Satan loves to waste Christian's efforts by giving to those he controls. He uses Christians to bring glory to himself and to keep Christians feeling good about themselves and their "good works."

I have spent hours listening to those who refused to come to the LORD and then wondered why I felt so depleted and discouraged. The LORD has shown me that this has to stop because I listen to Satan through them and he is the source of my disheartenment. I now try to listen to God within and when I do, He motivates me to stay or leave others without any guilt on my part. Those of Satan speak and do the things of Satan, the one in control of their heart.

God specifically asks me not to serve Satan—whether directly or indirectly through others. This I believe is a great misunderstanding in churches today. When Scripture refers to brethren or brothers, it means other committed believers. God never serves Satan and He will not in and through me.

God asks us to give our life to the brethren not to the world at large. We can do this because, if they are brethren, God is in charge of their life, so it is the same as giving our life to the LORD. God asks us to give our life to Him and Him only.

How can God ask us to give our life to those who have Satan in charge of their life? This would be asking us to serve Satan and this we know is not of God.

God's Spirit is resident in my heart. I am to guard this treasure—this pearl of great price.

Chapter 3: Living Grace: God's Expression In and Through Me

Once I am reassured of God reigning in my heart and motivating me, I follow my heart and allow God to express Himself in and through me.

A Life of Freedom

With God reigning in my heart, I am free from the law and all the "shoulds" I lived by for most of my life. I live in childlike dependency on my Father to lead me according to His will. I no longer struggle to know God's will. His will happens in and through me when I am in submission to Him.

When I let God reign in my life, I have a LIVING LORD and SAVIOR within. I am restored to the life Adam and Eve had in the Garden of Eden with God the Father. They did not need laws or authorities, because they knew only GOOD through their oneness with God the Father who is GOOD. Their choice was to listen and obey God the Father or go it alone by taking from the Tree of the Knowledge of Good and Evil. I, too, decide whether to cling to God, who is GOOD, or to revert to law which defines good and evil. I have to make God LORD of my life and give up being lord of my own life. Following GOOD is freedom from the law.

This is the FREEDOM Christ won for us.

> *For freedom Christ has set us free; stand fast therefore, and do not submit again to a yoke of slavery.*
>
> *Galatians 5:1*

Now the Lord is the Spirit, and where the Spirit of the Lord is, there is freedom. And we all, with unveiled face, beholding the glory of the Lord, are being changed into his likeness from one degree of glory to another; for this comes from the Lord who is the Spirit.

2 Corinthians 3:17-18

Freedom allows me to live like a child in the kingdom of God. God's kingdom is wherever God reigns and when He reigns in my heart, I am free. This is what Jesus was trying to tell us when He said:

Truly, I say to you, whoever does not receive the kingdom of God like a child shall not enter it.

Mark 10:15; Luke 18:17

When God reigns in my heart, I am free to express and follow my heart. It is no longer what should I do, but what God is motivating in me to do. I am free from the yoke of laws in my mind that define good and evil, because GOOD is in charge of my heart. It is no longer I, but Christ living in me.

Living in grace is our ultimate freedom.

Learning From My Own Words

One surprising aspect of God reigning in my life was hearing Him speak through me.

When I talk, I speak from my heart without censorship by my mind. Therefore, God has the opportunity to speak through me. I learn from what I say, because God is speaking and not me.

I hesitate to write this because it may sound presumptuous, but it is true. Anyone who walks in God's Spirit will understand. When God is in charge, He has access to our lips.

I hear wisdom coming from my lips that I did not know. I hear solutions to problems coming from my mouth that I know I did not figure out. I know that it is God speaking through me and not me.

When I listen and follow my heart, life becomes an exciting adventure because I do not know what God will do in a situation. While speaking to an audience or teaching a class, I was often pleasantly surprised by the words I spoke and how I learned from them. When I submit to God, He shows up and teaches not only the people I am speaking to, but me as well. Isn't that a wonderful win-win?

When I first realized that God was asking me to let Him live in and through me, I had enormous joy because I had been saved from myself. Christ was alive in me. I thank God for the times when my joy is inexpressible.

Eventually, however, I realized that God was not only going to do things I approved of but He was also going to rebuke others through me. I pondered how Jesus lived and wondered if God was going to speak through me as He did through Jesus. I was especially concerned about the rebukes that Jesus gave to the Pharisees calling them things such as hypocrites and sons of the devil.

I had to ask myself: Am I willing to speak truth even though the other person will not like me for saying it? Am I willing to say no when the other person expects me to say yes because of some belief system they live by? Am I willing to let God rebuke others through me? Am I willing to come away from someone God is asking me to separate from? These are the tests of my commitment to make God LORD of my life. Is my desire to please man greater than my desire to please God and obey Him? Am I willing to risk my reputation as a "nice" person? Am I willing to walk like Jesus walked in submission to the Father?

There is a down side to giving God control of our heart and lips. Often this keeps us from giving God control of our words. I never know what God will say through me and for someone who wants to make a good impression and not hurt anyone, this sometimes makes me uneasy. I trust Him, but there is still an element of wanting a bit more control over my words. I know that my Father knows what is best for me and for those who hear the words He speaks through me. Therefore, I am committed to allowing Him control over my words.

Sometimes people react to something I say and I have no idea what I said to get them stirred up. I have to trust that God knows what He is doing and He doesn't owe me an explanation of what He said or did. He does, however, seem willing to teach me what has happened if I ask for affirmation that it was of Him and not just my own response.

Occasionally I am so compelled to speak that I cannot hold in the words. It is as if God knows I am willing to speak but cautious to know that it is Him speaking. Most of the time, I have no hesitancy and just speak from my heart. Occasionally a situation makes me hesitate and God has to stoke up His energy within me until I feel I will burst if I don't speak. In this case, I know I will be disobedient if I do not say what He wants to say.

He rarely sends me to another person for the purpose of delivering a message to them. I just live my life committed to the LORD and whatever He speaks through me is His prerogative. I don't have any foreknowledge of what He intends to say. I don't expect to get prophetic words for others, because He can say it directly by bringing us together and then me just being myself. I am leery of those who "have a word from the Lord" for others. Perhaps I am too cautious but God doesn't need me to do His work. When He wants me involved He will let me know and cause it to happen. All I need to do is stay committed to heeding His promptings in me.

When others react unfavorably, I console myself that I did what God asked of me. I have no control over their reaction to what God says to them through me. Each of us chooses how we respond to God's words and are therefore responsible. I remember that Jesus said only what the Father said through Him and this is what I am to do. Jesus' words and actions were not always received; therefore, His words through me will not always be received favorably.

When I begin to waiver I remember that I am saved by believing in my heart and speaking with my lips.

*The word is near you, on your lips and in your heart (that is, the word of faith which we preach); because, **if you confess with your lips that Jesus is Lord and believe in your heart that God raised him from the dead, you will be saved. For man believes with his heart and so is justified, and he confesses with his lips and so is saved.** The scripture says, "No one who believes in him will be put to shame."* Romans 10:8-11

I am a learner and will make mistakes, but if I don't practice I will never live in grace.

Surprised By My Own Actions

When I gave God control of my life, He not only spoke through me, He began to act through me.

It was one thing for Him to speak through me and another thing for Him to prompt me to do a specific action. I am still too reserved about this and God is working with me.

Let me relate one incident that left a lasting impression on me of how God works through me when I allow Him to do so.

In a Bible Study someone began sharing her fears. I was listening and in my heart asking the Lord to meet her need. Suddenly I found myself on my feet and at a blackboard drawing a diagram showing the relationship of FEAR and FAITH to REPENTANCE.

FEAR		FAITH
Devil ———————————	———————————	God
Evil	**REPENT**	Good
	Turn Around	

This diagram was new to me and as I wrote it I was helped by it. I sat down and didn't think much more about this incident.

Later in her prayers, this same woman mentioned that she wished she had a better relationship with God. Suddenly I was back up on my feet and asking her to stand up. I asked her to repent and stop looking at Satan and evil and start looking at God and GOOD. She had been speaking about her fears and I was asking her to step into faith.

As we were standing there I noticed that a bright orange electric cord was below my feet and aligned directly with the REPENT—TURN AROUND words I had written on the board. So I asked her to step across this orange line.

What surprised me is that I had absolute faith that if she stepped across this line she would be saved from the oppression she was suffering. Even more incredible was the love I had for her.

Never had I experienced such faith and love before. I was not thinking about myself at all, I only had her welfare in my heart. I knew God had heard her prayer and was responding to her. I was overwhelmed by His love for her and His desire to answer her prayer.

Sadly, someone in the group was uncomfortable with what was going on, so the group leader stopped us before this lady had a chance to walk over the line.

So we sat down. I was thrilled at seeing God's love for this woman and His desire to answer her prayer. Surprisingly, I had no reaction to the leader who stopped us or to my own actions other than I knew God had showed up and chosen to work through me.

It wasn't until later, after being chastised by the leader, that I began to consider how this might have looked to those in the group. I tried to explain what had happened but I could tell the leader did not understand. Even though we were learning about prayer, she didn't expect God to show up and answer our prayers. I have to admit, I didn't expect Him to show up like that either, but I knew He had and no one will ever be able to take that away from me.

Later, as I discussed this incident and its ramifications with the LORD, the LORD showed me that I had experienced the fruits of His Spirit within me: love and faith. He went on to teach me that faith is a fruit of His Spirit and a gift of His Spirit. The same Greek word *pistis* is used for faith in the Scripture which identifies all the fruits of the Spirit as well as the Scripture listing the gifts of the Spirit. He showed me that this is the faith He looks for in His children.

As I reflect back on this incident, I know that it was God who motivated me to get up out of my chair and into action because I didn't particularly like this woman, yet the love I felt through me that night was immense. Of myself, I would never have done what I did. I have never done anything like this before and don't like to make a fool of myself. What really surprised me is that I never once worried how it looked to others as it happened or later. I was secure in knowing that God had showed up and I had been available. The results were up to Him because it was His work, not mine.

Jesus revealed to me that He would have been disheartened if He based His worth on the response of others. He based His life on how well He obeyed the Father. The response of others was their choice and responsibility. He showed me that my lack of regret over other's reactions was proof that this incident was of Him.

This experience taught me the difference between God's work and my work. My work is to believe in Him and be available to

Him. He does His work. *My Father doesn't "use" me to do His work; He reveals Himself to me by allowing me to experience Him doing His work through me.* Like Jesus' disciples, I am a learner.

I am getting a glimpse of what the author of Hebrews means when encouraging us to enter our Sabbath rest.

> *So then, there remains a sabbath rest for the people of God; for whoever enters God's rest also ceases from his labors as God did from his. Let us therefore strive to enter that rest, that no one fall by the same sort of disobedience.* Hebrews 4:9-11

What is the disobedience that keeps us from entering our Sabbath rest? He is referring to those who refuse to hear God's voice and obey Him — those who refuse to live in grace.

> *Therefore, as the Holy Spirit says, "Today, when you hear his voice, do not harden your hearts as in the rebellion, on the day of testing in the wilderness, where your fathers put me to the test and saw my works for forty years. Therefore I was provoked with that generation, and said, 'They always go astray in their hearts; they have not known my ways.' As I swore in my wrath, 'They shall never enter my rest.'" Take care, brethren, lest there be in any of you an evil, unbelieving heart, leading you to fall away from the living God.... So we see that they were unable to enter because of unbelief.* Hebrews 3:7-19

How do I enter this rest? I enter by heeding God's voice and promptings. Jesus lived in grace and demonstrated it for us. Now it is up to us to live in God's grace with God's Spirit influencing our heart and expressing Himself in and through us.

Prayer Became a Dialogue Rather Than a Monologue

I was not taught to expect God to talk with me, so my prayers were a monologue sent out into the air with a hope that God was listening and would do something. I never questioned this because all the people around me—my family, Christian leaders, and fellow church members—seemed to do the same thing. When we prayed together out loud, we were never silent waiting to hear God's voice. We never came together just to see what God wanted to say to us.

In the past I just said my prayers and hoped God would solve my problems. I abdicated my problems and life to Him. When I didn't see God answering them, I would take back control and solve it the best I could. I can point to a few answered prayers, but it was one of those roulette type of experiences.

When I gave my heart to the LORD, this changed. I began to hear God speaking to me. In my quiet times, I began to have dialogues with the LORD in which He would teach me and help me understand what He wanted from me. These are precious times and now I look forward to these times together each morning.

I now know why prayer had been a burden for me before and now is such a privilege. My prayers were based on hope instead of faith. I was hoping God would answer instead of expecting Him to show up. Now my prayers are relational, like a daughter and Father talking and sharing life with each other. Either one of us can initiate our dialogue.

Prayer has become more an ongoing communication with God's Spirit within me. I talk with Him continually as I go through my day. Sometimes it is asking for insights in my writing. Sometimes it is asking Him to show me the truth in situations. Sometimes I just praise Him for the beauty I see around me, and sometimes it is just appreciating my Father for who He is.

Prayer isn't always something initiated by me as it had been in the past. Sometimes God starts the conversation or motivates me to see or take some action. God's Spirit teaches me ALL things so He is active in me in whatever I do.

When I am reading, He highlights certain sentences or facts and motivates me to remember them. Sometimes He asks me to follow up on what He has shown me. Once while reading articles about Immunology, He highlighted a paragraph about Louis Pasteur and had me follow up by reading about His life and work. As a result, I learned that Pasteur is not the hero I once thought he was. I could write a book on what I learned about his character and experiments. On another occasion, it was the phrase "B-vitamins come from yeast" that caused me to do a research on yeast, which altered how I eat. Another time, it was the phrase "B-vitamins are formed from bacteria" that the Lord used to help me understand the detrimental effects of antibiotics.

I believe that God's Spirit teaches me everything I need to know. Scripture says "God's Spirit teaches us all things," but we don't take this seriously. When Scripture says we have no need that anyone teach us because the Spirit teaches us all things, we do not believe it.

Prayer is two-way. Prayer is a relationship, not a religious practice. Prayer never ceases when I am one with God's Spirit.

Instead of just speaking my prayers, I write them out because they are so meaningful and I want to remember what the LORD says to me. Although I still pray without writing, I prefer to write my prayers during my quiet time in the morning because of how much I treasure these times together with my Father.

I have written thousands of prayers and each time I reread them they touch my heart deeply and assure me that God has been in communion with me.

God Changed My Definition of "Life"

When I gave up control to the LORD, He changed me from the inside out.

First, I noticed that I lost interest in things that had been so important to me. I had many aspirations and values that were of the world and not of God. God began to purge these worldly values when I gave Him opportunity to do so.

I'll give you two examples. The first was my reputation. I have always been concerned about what others think of me and wanted them to like me. My reputation had been very important to me. When God got a hold of me, this diminished. I am not free of this desire but I know that I am much freer from this bondage than I have ever been.

The second example is my desire to be seen as a "good" Christian. As long as I had a great reputation in the church as an active member and leader, all was well. When God no longer allowed my participation in these ministries, some Christians began to question my commitment to the LORD. Initially this hurt, but God showed me through these experiences the futility of trying to please man and worrying about my reputation. I found freedom and greater opportunities to know God and follow Him. Being a nobody is part of the humbling process I needed.

We read in Scripture about the dying process but don't really understand until God begins this work in our life. We have to exchange our so-called life for His Life. We lose reputation, achievement, health, family, friends, wealth—whatever we base our worth and security in, so that He can be our all. God may give some of these blessings back but only if we keep them under His control and do not make them the basis of our life again.

As God takes worldly values out of my life, I feel like an outsider in this world. The Scripture that says we are "strangers and exiles" on the earth comes to mind. I often feel like an outsider even in my family and church. Those who live under the law have little affinity for me and me for them. I only feel at home with those who walk in God's Spirit and live in God's grace.

As I walk in God's grace, I am aware of how many people were in my life because I was a giver and they were takers. I now realize how many of them desired some control over my life and I was willing to let them influence me. Since I am learning to live in grace under God's divine influence, I see these takers and controllers gradually drift away because I can no longer give my life to them or allow them to control me.

I am surprised by the amount of unlearning I have to do. Because Satan is the ruler of this world, we pick up many lies. Those he controls spread his lies—often unknowingly. In science, medicine, history, psychology, or immunology, much of what we believe to be true is false. When I need to know truth in these areas, God is very willing to teach me what is true and to expose the falseness of my knowledge and beliefs.

Much of what we have been told and accepted as true is false, including much from our religious upbringing. God's Spirit within reveals truth and sets us free.

God takes us from the worldly systems we think are so valid into His spiritual kingdom. One example is the distinction between the organized church and the Body of Christ. Another example is the distinction between our earthly family and God's spiritual family. Scripture points us to the Body of Christ and our spiritual family but we hold on to these earthly relationships.

The degree to which I possess these worldly values is the degree to which I suffer when God cleanses them from my life.

Whatever we have in our life that keeps us from following the LORD, He attempts to cleanse from our life.

We lose reputation, a sense of accomplishment, family, friends, whatever we have our worth and security attached to. God wants us to do His work, and bring glory to His name, not for us to do our own works for our own glory. This is hard to accept in a world so geared to individual achievement and recognition. God also releases our grip on finances and the possessions we depend on for our security. He wants to be our security and worth.

As God gradually strips away what props us up, we have more and more of God. I take consolation in these words:

> *We have this treasure in earthen vessels, to show that* ***the transcendent power belongs to God and not to us***. *...* *For while we live we are always being given up to death for Jesus' sake,* ***so that the life of Jesus may be manifested in our mortal flesh***. *... So we do not lose heart. Though our outer nature is wasting away,* ***our inner nature is being renewed every day***. *For this slight momentary affliction is preparing for us an eternal weight of glory beyond all comparison, because we look not to the things that are seen but to the things that are unseen; for the things that are seen are transient, but the things that are unseen are eternal.*
>
> *2 Corinthians 4:7,11,16-18*

I find the following quote from Watchman Nee's *Christ The Sum Of All Spiritual Things* encouraging as losses take place in my life.

"How do I know I have died? How can I know that the cross has done its work in me? The answer is a simple one. If the Lord has worked in your life, you will lose many things. If you have stayed in tact since you were saved, you being as rich and as full as before then this plainly indicates that the cross has not worked in you. As the cross operates in our life, you will notice what a big subtracting or cleansing work the Lord has accomplished in you. As a consequence, what you were able to do before you are now no longer able. What you once were confident of, you presently are not so confident of; and what you originally had great courage in, you lately are hesitant about."

As God does His cleansing and renewing, many beliefs and traditions I once held sacred were challenged and redefined.

Our parents are responsible to bring us to the Lord, not to possess us and bring us to themselves and their beliefs. Often parents become obstacles to their children coming to the LIVING LORD by keeping them tied to some particular denomination that doesn't recognize our LIVING LORD and SAVIOR.

God showed me that earthly families can be in close relationship only if all come to the LORD and follow HIM. When some refuse to come to the LORD, divisions and conflicts cannot be averted.

God showed me that my tradition of belonging to a church organization is not belonging to His Body. His Body are those who listen to His voice and obey. Church organizations have both sheep—God's children—and wolves—Satan followers.

As I was going through losses trying desperately to hold on to what I thought was life, I did suffer and shed many tears. It was not until I came through the fire that I could see what God had done in my life. By remembering each loss and each gain from it, I get better equipped to persevere through new losses.

As in the past, I am sure I will question God why this is happening to me. I hope I will remember the great freedom that comes from losses. Hopefully this will help me hold on long enough to see the victory and overcome my hesitancy to let go.

God purges these things from my life so He can replace them with His Life.

Paul said it well with:

> *I have been crucified with Christ;* ***it is no longer I who*** ***live, but Christ who lives in me****; and the life I now live in the flesh I live by faith in the Son of God, who loved me and gave himself for me. I do not nullify the grace of God; for if justification were through the law, then Christ died to no purpose.*   *Galatians 2:20-21*

> *Whatever gain I had, I counted as loss for the sake of Christ. Indeed I count everything as loss because of the* ***surpassing worth of knowing Christ Jesus my Lord****. For his sake I have suffered the loss of all things, and count them as refuse, in order that* ***I may gain Christ*** ***and be found in him****, not having a righteousness of my own, based on law, but that which is through faith in Christ, the righteousness from God that depends on faith.*   *Philippians 3:7-9*

> ***For to me to live is Christ, and to die is gain.***
> *Philippians 1:21*

Learning to walk in God's grace has been worth the cost. Grace is truly the pearl of great price and worth losing all my worldly life. Living in grace is living as Jesus lived.

Chapter 4: Law-Based Christians Persecute Believers Living In Grace

One surprise of living in God's grace is the reaction of law-based Christians. They will not only question your faith, but also defame your name and persecute you.

Jesus Was Persecuted By Law-Based Religious People

Why this occurs is made clear by the reaction of the Pharisees to Jesus. Law-based churchgoers respond to the living Savior in us the same way. So let's look at the Pharisee's response to Jesus.

> *The Pharisees went out and took counsel against him, how to destroy him. Jesus, aware of this, withdrew from there.*   *Matthew 12:14-15*

> *When the Pharisees heard it they said, "It is only by Beelzebul, the prince of demons, that this man casts out demons."*   *Matthew 12:24*

> *The Pharisees and Sadducees came, and to test him they asked him to show them a sign from heaven.*
>   *Matthew 16:1*

> *Then the Pharisees went and took counsel how to entangle him in his talk.*   *Matthew 22:15*

> *The chief priests and the elders of the people gathered in the palace of the high priest, who was called Caiaphas, and took counsel together in order to arrest Jesus by stealth and kill him.*   *Matthew 26:3-4*

The chief priests and the whole council sought false testimony against Jesus that they might put him to death.

Matthew 26:59

The chief priests and the elders persuaded the people to ask for Barabbas and destroy Jesus.   Matthew 27:20

I included here only a few references from Matthew that illustrate the Pharisee's and religious leader's response to Jesus. There are many references in the New Testament describing the persecution of Jesus by religious leaders and their followers. I highlighted them in my Bible to remind me that I can expect no less if Christ is in me.

We know too that these religious leaders were the instigators behind Jesus being tortured and crucified on the cross. When Pilate wanted to release Jesus, the chief priests and officers cried out:

"We have a law and by that law he ought to die, because he has made himself the Son of God."   John 19:7

Religious people live by the law and want to control others by the law. Jesus' life and message threatened their positions of power and prestige.

*So the chief priests and the Pharisees gathered the council, and said, "What are we to do? For this man performs many signs. If we let him go on thus, every one will believe in him, and the Romans will come and **destroy both our holy place and our nation**."*

John 11:47-48

Coming out from under the law threatens authorities that derive their positions based on laws. This includes leaders in religious organizations who have their positions of authority and status based on control over their organizations.

Today church pastors and elders do not stand up to the heads of their church organizations for fear of losing their power and authority. Heads of Christian organizations do not stand up against perversion because the government might take away their tax-exemption.

Jesus understood that He would suffer at the hands of religious leaders.

From that time Jesus began to show his disciples that he must go to Jerusalem and suffer many things from the elders and chief priests and scribes, and be killed.
Matthew 16:21

Elders and chief priests are the religious leaders of Jesus' day persecuting Him and seeking to destroy Him. With Christ in us and living in grace, we too can expect the same reaction from law-based Christians and leaders today. Grace and law are incompatible. Jesus warned us about persecution from law-based religious leaders:

Remember the word that I said to you, 'A servant is not greater than his master.' **If they persecuted me, they will persecute you***; if they kept my word, they will keep yours also.* *John 15:20*

If they have called the master of the house Beelzebul, **how much more will they malign those of his household.** *Matthew 10:25*

Jesus' Disciples Were Persecuted by Law-Based Religious People

Jesus' disciples met opposition and persecution for their faith in a living Lord within them—for living in grace.

Peter and John met opposition immediately when God's Spirit began to work through them. The priests and leaders of the temple arrested them and warned them not to speak in the name of Jesus. Repeatedly they were arrested and put in prison by law-based zealots who warned them not to teach in His name.

Paul, as a Pharisee, was one of these law-based religious zealots. He persecuted those who lived in grace, that is, those who expressed Christ in them.

Christ's words to Paul at his conversion are telling.

> *"Saul, Saul, why do you persecute me?" And he said, "Who are you, Lord?" And he said, "I am Jesus, whom you are persecuting."* Acts 9:4-5

Jesus made it clear that Paul was persecuting Christians because Christ was in them.

Law-based religious people will persecute anyone who is a true disciple of Christ living in grace.

Paul Was Persecuted by Law-Based Religious People

When Paul became a believer, he too suffered persecution from religious zealots. These zealots pursued him from town to town and drove him out of their synagogues.

Paul, however, understood that he would be persecuted for his walk of grace. God's Spirit within him warned him.

> *The **Holy Spirit** testifies to me in every city that imprisonment and afflictions await me. But I do not account my life of any value nor as precious to myself, if only I may accomplish my course and the ministry which I received from the Lord Jesus, to testify to the gospel of the grace of God.* Acts 20:23-24

While studying persecution of believers in the book of Acts, I was amazed to find that religious leaders persecuted every early disciple of Christ.

Stephen Was Persecuted by Law-Based Religious People

The account about Stephen sums up the persecution we can expect when we are true believers.

> *Stephen, **full of grace and power**, did great wonders and signs among the people. **Then some of those who belonged to the synagogue...arose and disputed with Stephen. But they could not withstand the wisdom and the Spirit with which he spoke. Then they secretly instigated men,** who said, "We have heard him speak blasphemous words against Moses and God." And **they stirred up the people and the elders and the scribes, and they came upon him and seized him and brought him before the council, and set up false witnesses** who said, "This man never ceases to speak words against this holy place and the law; for we have heard him say that this Jesus of Nazareth will destroy this place, and will change the customs which Moses delivered to us."*
>
> *Acts 6:8-14*

Stephen, full of grace and the Spirit with which he spoke threatened those who had their holy place and the law. They didn't want their laws and customs changed.

We Will Be Persecuted by Law-Based Religious People

Grace and law are not compatible. Those who choose to live in grace will be persecuted by those who choose law.

I say this to warn you because when persecution started happening to my husband and I, we became discouraged and started to wonder if we were following Christ. It was only God's grace within that spared us from succumbing to the pressures of law-based church-goers.

We found that law-based church-goers can be vehement and self-righteous defending their beliefs and laws. Should you question their actions, they can get hostile.

Satan can deceive us into believing that we are on the right path by studying Scriptures and trying to live by what is written there. Many zealous Christians in their desire to do what is right become Bible worshippers and doers of good works. These are the most upset when they encounter a Christian who lives in grace because it calls into question their faith and threatens the way they live. In their mind either they are right and you are wrong or you are right and they are wrong. They live at the Tree of The Knowledge of Good and Evil and, therefore, have not yet entered grace. Living in grace is a threat to them. As a result, they distrust you, reject you, get others to reject you, and eventually ostracize you.

Don't be surprised if you are dismissed or rejected by those who sit in the pews next to you. This will be one of the hard tests to see how committed you are to following the LORD. Those who cling to law and self-righteousness are fearful of those who live in grace and will react to you in hurtful ways. The spiritual battle becomes intense when we make our commitment to the LORD and come out of this world. We come out from under the laws that earthly organizations value and rely on.

Committing to the LORD will reveal those who try to keep one foot in God's kingdom and one in the world. God's Spirit in you will conflict with those who try to look good on the outside by their religious practices but are still of the world. God's Spirit will show you who are the takers and controllers in your life as He takes you out from under them.

You may be rejected by your religious family for not conforming to their beliefs and traditions. Your freedom in Christ will conflict with those who are law-based and committed to beliefs and traditions rather than to the LORD. Families, like any organization, will not give up their control over you without conflicts and rejection.

Others will not understand and may judge you as radical. Family and friends may leave you. The church may consider you dangerous. This is *the cross* that you must bear. Remember, you have Christ within and He is the same today, yesterday and tomorrow. If Christ is reflected in your life, the world will have the same response to you as it did to Him. Are you willing to suffer for Christ's sake?

> *Then Jesus told his disciples, "**If any man would come after me, let him deny himself and take up his cross and follow me.**"*   *Matthew 16:24*

> *"Do not think that I have come to bring peace on earth; I have not come to bring peace, but a sword. For I have come to set a man against his father, and a daughter against her mother, and a daughter-in-law against her mother-in-law; and a man's foes will be those of his own household. He who loves father or mother more than me is not worthy of me; and he who loves son or daughter more than me is not worthy of me; and **he who does not take his cross and follow me is not worthy of me**. He who finds his life will lose it, and he who loses his life for my sake will find it. He who receives you receives me, and he who receives me receives him who sent me."*   *Matthew 10:34-40*

> *"**If any man would come after me, let him deny himself and take up his cross daily and follow me.** For whoever would save his life will lose it; and whoever loses his life for my sake, he will save it. For what does it profit a man if he gains the whole world and loses or forfeits himself? For whoever is ashamed of me and of my words, of him will the Son of man be ashamed when he comes in his glory and the glory of the Father and of*

the holy angels. But I tell you truly, there are some standing here who will not taste death before they see the kingdom of God." Luke 9:23-27

"If any one comes to me and does not hate his own father and mother and wife and children and brothers and sisters, yes, and even his own life, he cannot be my disciple. **Whoever does not bear his own cross and come after me, cannot be my disciple.** *For which of you, desiring to build a tower, does not first sit down and count the cost, whether he has enough to complete it? Otherwise, when he has laid a foundation, and is not able to finish, all who see it begin to mock him, saying, 'This man began to build, and was not able to finish.' Or what king, going to encounter another king in war, will not sit down first and take counsel whether he is able with ten thousand to meet him who comes against him with twenty thousand? And if not, while the other is yet a great way off, he sends an embassy and asks terms of peace. So therefore,* **whoever of you does not renounce all that he has cannot be my disciple."** Luke 14:26-33

We must be willing to pay the cost of following Jesus, living as He did. God's Spirit within reveals the heart of others and if not of God, conflicts will inevitably follow.

Don't be alarmed. Remember when you too thought that Bible verses were going to save you. Yes, save you. If you are genuinely honest with yourself, you know that there is some truth to this. Remember when you thought your security was your family. God replaces our definition of life with His Life.

All Christians who don't hear the voice of the LIVING God within have to live by the law. The Bible is their only recourse for knowing what to do and how to live. Therefore, Scripture becomes their god and they worship the words written there rather than the LIVING God within them. Many Christians think they have no need to hear God because God recorded all they need to know in the Bible.

In His rebuke of the Pharisees, Jesus warned them against searching Scriptures to obtain eternal life. Today Christians search the Scriptures continually yet fail to see that they point to a LIVING SAVIOR. Jesus puts it even stronger, He rebukes them for refusing to come to Him.

> *You search the scriptures, because you think that in them you have eternal life; and it is they that bear witness to me; yet you refuse to come to me that you may have life.*
> *John 5:39-40*

Yes, we can refuse to come to the LORD even though the Bible clearly points to the work of God's Spirit within each believer. We refuse because man's sinful nature wants to be in control and it is easier to check off Bible verses to see how we are doing rather than giving up our life to God's divine influence within.

Some church-goers and Bible-worshippers may not even have God's divine influence within because they, like Adam and Eve, want to know good and evil to make decisions on their own. They want their own righteousness. They are what the Bible refers to as the self-righteous—the Pharisees of today.

The Bible is meant to bring us to Christ, not replace Him with beliefs and laws. Jesus is the WORD, the living WORD made flesh.

Our Response to Persecution—Living In Grace

One of the most important aspects of living in grace is to test the spirit of others.

> *Beloved, **do not believe every spirit, but test the spirits to see whether they are of God**; for many false prophets have gone out into the world. By this you know the Spirit of God: every spirit which **confesses** that Jesus Christ*

*has come in the flesh is of God, and every spirit which does not **confess** Jesus is not of God. This is the spirit of antichrist, of which you heard that it was coming, and now it is in the world already. Little children, you are of God, and have overcome them; for he who is in you is greater than he who is in the world. They are of the world, therefore what they say is of the world, and the world listens to them. We are of God. **Whoever knows God listens to us, and he who is not of God does not listen to us. By this we know the spirit of truth and the spirit of error.** 1 John 4:1-6*

Just by living in grace—allowing God to speak through us—we can see how others respond. Those of God will listen to God speaking through us, those not of God will not listen for they still are of the world and therefore listen to the world and not to God.

The word "confess" in the above Scripture comes from the Greek word *homologeo*, a combination of *homo* which means "together" and *logos* which means "something said." In combination, they mean something said together. I interpret this to mean a child of God allows God to speak through him. This is how Jesus lived with God speaking and working through Him.

As with Jesus, others will react to God's words through us and to our claiming to be sons and daughters of God. Living in grace, with the Spirit of God within us, exposes false Christians.

Testing the spirit of others is one of the ways God keeps us from inadvertently trying to have fellowship with those that would persecute us. Some persecution can be avoided by taking note of how others respond to what God is saying through us. Some harm can be averted by following His promptings from within as He leads us away from dangers.

Persecution, however, cannot be avoided because we live in this world. Attacks and rejections will surely come.

Be prepared to stand when these attacks come and remember that God's Spirit is in you as He was in Jesus. When you allow His divine influence on your life you are prepared to handle these rejections and abuses. God will speak to you and comfort you. He will speak through you to those who accuse you.

> *"Take heed to yourselves; for they will deliver you up to councils; and you will be beaten in synagogues; and you will stand before governors and kings for my sake, to bear testimony before them.... And when they bring you to trial and deliver you up, do not be anxious beforehand what you are to say; but say whatever is given you in that hour, for it is not you who speak, but the Holy Spirit."*   *Mark 13:9-11*

Scripture warns us about those who would lord it over us with laws and authority.

When persecutions come, we are not to respond in like kind. We are to rely on our Father to fight for us. This may be with or without our participation.

> **Repay no one evil for evil**, *but take thought for what is noble in the sight of all. If possible, so far as it depends upon you, live peaceably with all. Beloved,* **never avenge yourselves***, but leave it to the wrath of God; for it is written, "Vengeance is mine, I will repay, says the Lord."*   *Romans 12:17-19*

God desires that all come to know Him. Our life living in grace is a testimony and witness to law-based church-goers. If they repent and come to the LIVING SAVIOR, they are saved. If they refuse, God may speak a message of truth through you that they need to hear.

Jesus' Response to Law-Based Religious People

Look at the messages God spoke through Jesus when the Pharisees attacked Him.

"Woe to you, scribes and Pharisees, hypocrites! because you shut the kingdom of heaven against men; for you neither enter yourselves, nor allow those who would enter to go in. Woe to you, scribes and Pharisees, hypocrites! for you traverse sea and land to make a single proselyte, and when he becomes a proselyte, you make him twice as much a child of hell as yourselves."

Matthew 23:13-15

"Woe to you, scribes and Pharisees, hypocrites! for you tithe mint and dill and cummin, and have neglected the weightier matters of the law, justice and mercy and faith; these you ought to have done, without neglecting the others. You blind guides, straining out a gnat and swallowing a camel!"   *Matthew 23:23-24*

"Woe to you, scribes and Pharisees, hypocrites! for you cleanse the outside of the cup and of the plate, but inside they are full of extortion and rapacity. You blind Pharisee! first cleanse the inside of the cup and of the plate, that the outside also may be clean.   "

Matthew 23:25-26

"Woe to you, scribes and Pharisees, hypocrites! for you are like whitewashed tombs, which outwardly appear beautiful, but within they are full of dead men's bones and all uncleanness. So you also outwardly appear righteous to men, but within you are full of hypocrisy and iniquity."   *Matthew 23:27-28*

"You seek to kill me, because my word finds no place in you. I speak of what I have seen with my Father, and you

do what you have heard from your father." They
answered him, "Abraham is our father..."Jesus said to
them, "If God were your Father, you would love me, for
I proceeded and came forth from God; I came not of my
own accord, but he sent me. Why do you not understand
what I say? It is because you cannot bear to hear my
word. You are of your father the devil, and your will is to
do your father's desires.... He who is of God hears the
words [rhema] of God; the reason why you do not hear
them is that you are not of God."   *John 8:40-47*

I don't want to say these kinds of things to anyone, yet alone
someone who calls himself Christian. Yet, Jesus, our role model,
did say these things to law-based religious leaders.

Jesus is the same yesterday, today, and tomorrow. Will He
conduct Himself any differently in us than He did when on
earth?

We are to live as Jesus did. We are changed into His image.
Therefore, we must be committed to do as He did. *God's Spirit
in Jesus is the same Spirit in us.* We are the temple of the living
God and from His temple He speaks. Therefore, let us take heed
and know our LIVING LORD and SAVIOR intimately and then
we will obey His commands when He chooses to use us to speak
to another.

Beware of Law-Based Religious Leaders

Pharisees held their positions of authority because of their study
and understanding of the law. To undermine the law was a threat
to their positions.

Leaders in the organized church today also obtain positions from
their knowledge of the Bible, not necessarily from their
relationship with God. Bible knowledge and theological degrees

are the prerequisite to be a pastor. The higher the academic degree the more prestige and salary they receive.

True ministers of God speak God's words from His Spirit within them. These messages contain fresh revelation from God and penetrate the open hearts of those who hear them.

Paul understood this and relied on God's Spirit speaking through him and not on his religious education. He knew that the written law kills but the Spirit gives life. He understood that his job was to demonstrate the power of God's Spirit, not his knowledge of Scripture or his ability to speak.

> *Not that we are competent of ourselves to claim anything as coming from us; our competence is from God, who has made us competent to be ministers of a new covenant, not in a written code but in the Spirit; for the written code kills, but the Spirit gives life.*
>
> *2 Corinthians 3:5-6*

> *When I came to you, brethren, **I did not come proclaiming to you the testimony of God in lofty words or wisdom**. For I decided to know nothing among you except Jesus Christ and him crucified. And I was with you in weakness and in much fear and trembling; and **my speech and my message were not in plausible words of wisdom, but in demonstration of the Spirit and of power, that your faith might not rest in the wisdom of men but in the power of God.*** *1 Corinthians 2:1-5*

Today pastors are hired for their ability to preach good sermons and for their academic credentials. There is often little or no assessment of their spiritual condition. Those responsible to select pastoral candidates often do not know how to assess the spirit of another because they themselves do not hear God's Spirit within their hearts.

Religious leaders can be threatened when the Bible cannot be used to maintain their authority over members of their churches. Growing the size of their organization is a prime focus of many churches. Evangelism to many pastors and leaders of church organizations means greater prestige for them and increased salaries. Tithing, emphasized as a law of blessing, means greater funds for their programs and salaries.

Look behind the scenes of churches today and you will find little discipleship, entertaining videos, and fill-in-the-blank Bible studies. Members are seen as free volunteer laborers to support the church's programs.

This seems harsh, but by living in grace you will see truth and be set free from these false authorities that would use you and care little about you. What makes us think that the law-based religious leaders today are any different from the Pharisees of Jesus' day? Why do we choose to ignore the numerous warnings in the Bible about this?

We are asked to obey those who are over us "in the LORD."

> *We beseech you, brethren, to respect those who labor among you and are over you **in the Lord** and admonish you, and to esteem them very highly in love because of their work.* 1 Thessalonians 5:12-13

Many religious leaders are not "in the Lord" because they are not submitted to the LORD and living in grace.

We've already seen what Jesus thought of the religious leaders of His day. Paul, too, had to warn believers about false authorities.

> *What I do I will continue to do, in order to undermine the claim of those who would like to claim that in their boasted mission they work on the same terms as we do. For such men are **false apostles, deceitful workmen, disguising themselves as apostles of Christ**. And no*

wonder, for even Satan disguises himself as an angel of light. So it is not strange if his servants also disguise themselves as servants of righteousness.... For you bear it if a man makes slaves of you, or preys upon you, or takes advantage of you, or puts on airs, or strikes you in the face. 2 Corinthians 11:12-20

*I am astonished that you are so quickly deserting him who called you in the grace of Christ and turning to a different gospel—not that there is another gospel, but **there are some who trouble you and want to pervert the gospel of Christ**.... If I were still pleasing men, I should not be a servant of Christ. For I would have you know, brethren, that the gospel which was preached by me is not man's gospel. For I did not receive it from man, nor was I taught it, but it came through a revelation of Jesus Christ.* Galatians 1:6-12

*For we are not, like so many, **peddlers of God's word**; but as men of sincerity, as commissioned by God, in the sight of God we speak in Christ.* 2 Corinthians 2:17

Paul calls them peddlers of the word. Not many pastors these days preach current revelation from the LORD. Most sermons are rehashed Bible verses.

Often church leaders will rebuke you for hearing God and walking in God's Spirit because they are unwilling to bear the cross of Christ within. They desire you to follow them and contribute to their programs which often have little to do with bringing others to Christ. In the following verse, the circumcism law is discussed, but today it could be tithing or church attendance. Paul is reminding us that we too must be crucified to the world for the sake of Christ and have faith to resist the imploring of church Pharisees to get back under the law.

*It is those who want to **make a good showing in the flesh** that would compel you to be circumcised, and only **in order that they may not be persecuted for the cross of Christ**. For even those who receive circumcision do not themselves keep the law, but they desire to have you circumcised that they may glory in your flesh. But far be it from me to glory except in the cross of our Lord Jesus Christ, by which the world has been crucified to me, and I to the world. For neither circumcision counts for anything, nor uncircumcision, but a new creation.*

Galatians 6:12-15

The Pharisees and other church leaders were trying to get believers back under the law in order to make a good showing and keep their positions. Many pastors today are not willing to stand up against evils under the guise of tolerance. Churches now allow those engaged in adultery and perversion to be their pastors and elders.

When you question their decisions, you will be condemned for judging and lack of tolerance. They will use selected Bible verses to convince themselves they are right and ignore other Bible verses that clearly warn believers about adultery and perversion.

Therefore, anyone living in grace and having God's Spirit speaking through them can expect to be rejected and abused.

Living In Grace Is Not the Easy Path, But the Only WAY

When we live in grace, with God's divine influence upon our heart, our life will conflict with those who still live under the law.

We must learn to listen and follow the LORD *before* listening and following man. We become God-pleasers not man-pleasers.

Those who are in the flesh cannot please God. But you are not in the flesh, you are in the Spirit, if in fact the Spirit of God dwells in you.   *Romans 8:8-9*

We speak, not to please men, but to please God who tests our hearts.   *1 Thessalonians 2:4*

If I were still pleasing men, I should not be a servant of Christ.   *Galatians 1:10*

Our very life will be a testimony against those who rely on their beliefs and laws to save them. Therefore, do not be disheartened when you are accused and rejected for not conforming.

Don't be surprised when you give your life to the LORD and suddenly you are at odds with people you formerly had a good relationship with. God's Spirit in you is not in harmony with Satan's spirit in another. You have changed and your relationship with those who have yet to come to Christ will change. It is the spirit in them that resists the Spirit in you. For Satan and his demons know the Spirit of God and are opposed to obeying God in any way.

As you begin your commitment to the kingdom of God within, others will try to have you follow them because this is the only way Satan within them can be around you. They cannot follow Christ within you while they hold to their independence from God and thus serve the evil one. You cannot follow them because God's Spirit within you cannot follow Satan in them. This causes great pain and suffering especially if these are loved ones or friends. This is the cross we are to bear.

I had a much different view of what following Christ would mean. I thought I would have better relationships with others because I was cleaning up my act and that others had already done so. But as I live this walk, the LORD reveals to me the condition of many Christians. He has shown me that many are today's Pharisees and that they will react to His presence in me the same way they reacted to Him. So be forewarned that this walk in God's Spirit is not what you may have imagined it to be.

Know that God's power overcomes our weakness. My weakness of wanting to be liked by everyone had to go. Even my desire to be with people I loved had to undergo great changes.

It is easier to go along with the prevailing winds and not stir up anyone. With God's Spirit in us, this will no longer be possible because God's Spirit within you speaks truth through you. God's Spirit through us convicts.

For the word of God is living and active, sharper than any two-edged sword, piercing to the division of soul and spirit, of joints and marrow, and discerning the thoughts and intentions of the heart. *Hebrews 4:12*

God's Spirit and His living, present tense, voice through our lips convicts and opposes the evil one directly and those he controls.

*And take the helmet of salvation, and **the sword of the Spirit, which is the word** [rhema—living word] **of God**.*
Ephesians 6:17

Why do we think we can escape persecution when Jesus was persecuted and warns us that it will be the same for us? I believe it is because we think we can avoid conflicts by giving in to those under the law. We are deceived into thinking that law and grace can coexist. We are deceived into thinking that Satan's spirit in another can be in harmony with God's Spirit in us.

When we put pleasing others above pleasing God, we turn away from the LORD within to please man without. Without realizing it, we SIN by separating ourselves from God. We return to the enemy's domain.

Choosing to follow Christ is to live in grace and accept suffering along with Him. This is why Scripture advises us to consider the cost.

Whoever does not bear his own cross and come after me, cannot be my disciple. For which of you, desiring to build a tower, does not first sit down and count the cost, whether he has enough to complete it? Otherwise, when he has laid a foundation, and is not able to finish, all who see it begin to mock him, saying, 'This man began to build, and was not able to finish....'" So therefore, whoever of you does not renounce all that he has cannot be my disciple.   *Luke 14:27-33*

We are to be witnesses by living Christ and allowing God's Spirit within us to reign. Nothing should detour us from living in grace.

We saw how Jesus dealt with law-based religious leaders and we too will find God's Spirit in us speaking out against these so-called Christians.

As we live in grace, we come out from under the law and the authorities that rule by the law. We become confident in our walk in God's Spirit only as we listen and obey—as we are led by God's Spirit.

God does not reside in a building or in those who glory in their Bible knowledge and positions of authority in the organized church. God is only in those who allow His Spirit to reign in their heart. These alone are the Body of Christ—the temple of our LIVING LORD.

So interpreting grace as merely unmerited favor can be a deception to keep us from entering the gift of God's grace.

Our commitment has to be to give up our life to God's influence upon our heart and His expression in our life. This is living in grace by FAITH. This is BELIEVING in Him whom He has sent. This is our SALVATION.

About the Author

Carolyn Bardsley studied Scripture for most of her adult life. Over time she realized she had considerable head knowledge but little heart connection to her Lord. This troubled her when she read Jesus' rebuke of the Pharisees for their knowledge of Scripture, yet refusing to come to Him—a LIVING SAVIOR. She was also troubled by the commandment to love the Lord because how could she love someone without having her heart engaged? Having been taught to distrust her heart, this dilemma caused her to study what Scripture said about the heart and mind which revealed the importance of *believing in our heart*.

In the 1980s Carolyn developed and taught a gifts and calling workshop for churches. Since Carolyn had developed and taught career and life planning workshops in corporations, she had a unique perspective on how spiritual gifts relate to motivations and skills in jobs and careers. In these workshops she saw how many people were disconnected from their hearts. She could identify with them having lived in her mind for most of her life.

In the 1990s Carolyn realized that God wants to talk with people today. While studying Scripture about hearing God, she was surprised to find that hearing God's voice was a function of the heart. *"Today, when you hear his voice do not harden your hearts." "Believe in your heart."* Knowing that as a believer she had the Spirit of the LIVING GOD in her heart, she began to trust that God would speak to her if she trusted in His presence in her. Daily quiet time became a conversation with the Lord. Scripture became a pointer to a LIVING LORD and SAVIOR—

not just a biography about Him. Her faith became one of believing in her heart because God's Spirit resides there.

During a time of illness she sought to understand how God provided comfort during suffering. The Scripture *"My grace is sufficient for you, for my strength is made perfect in weakness,"* prompted her to look up what grace meant. Grace as "God's unmerited favor" did not console her. Her grace study, using Scripture and *Strong's Greek Concordance,* dramatically changed her understanding of grace. She writes about her new understanding of grace in her books *Grace* and *Living In Grace.*

Her discovery about the importance of heart faith and living in grace has been so profound in her own walk of faith that she joys to share it with others to strengthen their faith in a LIVING LORD AND SAVIOR who seek to have a heart relationship with them.

Notes

Notes

Notes

Notes

Notes

Notes

Made in the USA
Charleston, SC
01 October 2016